Colorado
Easy & Scenic
Hikes

Dave Muller

Westcliffe Publishers
BOULDER

Sep 2013

Copyright © 2013 by Dave Muller

Published by Westcliffe Publishers
a Big Earth Publishing company
3005 Center Green Drive, Suite 225
Boulder, Colorado 80301
1-800-258-5830
E-mail: books@bigearthpublishing.com
www.bigearthpublishing.com

Cover and text design: D. Kari Luraas
Cover photos: D. Kari Luraas
Maps: D. Kari Luraas
Production Manager: Mira Perrizo
Editorial Assistant: Lauren Szenina
Cover: The Loch and the Sharkstooth beyond in Rocky Mountain National Park

9   8   7   6   5   4   3   2   1

Library of Congress Control Number: 2013942320
ISBN 978-1-56579-660-7

Printed in Korea

Please Note: Risk is always a factor in backcountry and high-mountain travel. Many of the activities described in this book can be dangerous, especially when weather is adverse or unpredictable, and when unforeseen events or conditions create a hazardous situation. The author has done his best to provide the reader with accurate information about backcountry travel, as well as to point out some of its potential hazards. It is the responsibility of the users of this guide to learn the necessary skills for safe backcountry travel, and to exercise caution in potentially hazardous areas, especially on glaciers and avalanche-prone terrain. The author and publisher disclaim any liability for injury or other damage caused by backcountry traveling or performing any other activity described in this book.

Contents

Acknowledgments

Let me bless and thank the many persons who encouraged and brought this book into being:

The Source of the Universe has endowed Colorado and its beauties with so much to be grateful for.

My wife, Jackie, has been an ally and source of inspiration for over fifty-three years.

My hiking companions have promoted fellowship and good conversation.

And the wonderful people at Big Earth Publishing—Linda Doyle, Susan Bhat, Mira Perrizo, and Kari Luraas—who were a delight to work with.

Introduction

This is the perfect hiking guide for those who enjoy hiking in the beauty of the Colorado Mountains without great exertion. High, rugged peaks and long treks can be wonderful, but often the easier destinations get overlooked. Families with children, seniors, and persons with disabilities especially need a selection of hikes that enable them to experience some of the beauty of this state.

The terms easy and scenic are of course subjective. These are some of the better, gentler outings that the author has experienced.

Order of Hikes: The hikes in this book are listed arbitrarily in order of increasing difficulty. The first is the easiest and the last is the most demanding. All hikes are less than four miles each way, with an occasional exception, and less than 2,000 feet of elevation gain.

Hiking Times: These are times of the author over the past decades. They are listed to provide points of reference only.

Elevation Gain: This figure includes elevation losses on the ascent as the trail declines and some ascending parts of the trail on the descent. Those are the extra feet that are included.

Relevant Maps: The most useful usually is the Trails Illustrated Map. The greatest detail is provided by the 7½ minute U.S.G.S. Maps. The schematic map with each hike will usually suffice.

Caution: Mountain terrain can be dangerous with falls, bad weather, and getting lost. Be sure to carry a compass, adequate water, clothing, a cell phone if possible, and a map. Leave word with someone about your destination and anticipated time of return.

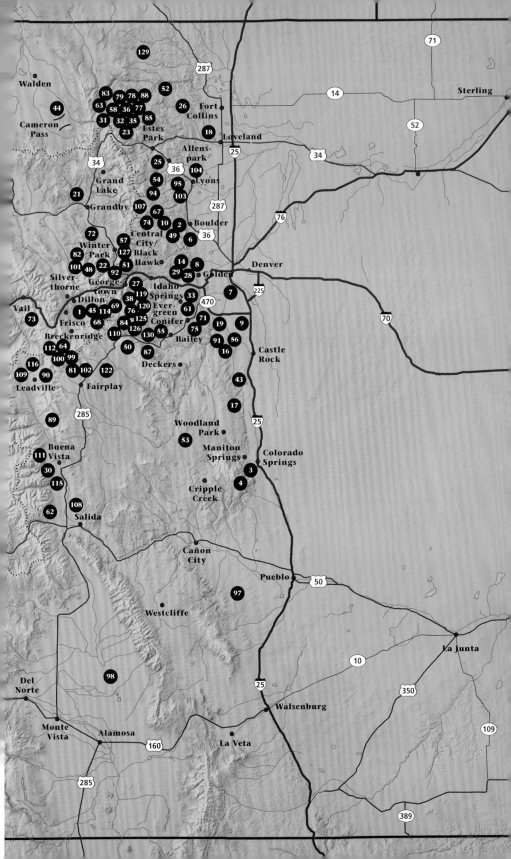

1 Old Dillon Reservoir

Here is a short, scenic hike to the Old Dillon Reservoir between Lake Dillon and I-70. The good views from the ridge in the middle part of this hike are special. Buffalo Mountain, Torreys Peak, Grays Peak, Mount Guyot, Bald Mountain, and the Tenmile Range encircle the trail in the distance.

Getting There: Drive south from Exit 203 of I-70 west of Dillon, and within 100 yards turn left onto the frontage road, also called Dam Road. Follow this paved road to the northeast for 1.8 miles and turn left into the parking area at the Old Dillon Reservoir Trailhead.

The Hike: Begin to the west-northwest from the trailhead sign and follow the good trail up to a ridge. Lake Dillon is impressive on the right. Follow the ridge down to the former reservoir and avoid a trail descending on the left from the ridge. A trail encircles the reservoir over 0.3 mile and connects back to the ridge trail and the trailhead.

Hike Distance: 0.6 mile each way

Hiking Time: Up in 13 minutes. Down in 11 minutes

Starting Elevation: 9,080 feet

Highest Elevation: 9,300 feet

Elevation Gain: 325 feet (includes 105 extra feet)

Trail: All the way

Relevant Maps: Trails Illustrated 108

    Frisco 7½ minute

    Summit County Number Two

    Arapaho National Forest—Dillon Ranger District

View from Old Dillion Reservoir trail over Lake Dillion to Mount Guyot and Bald Mountain.

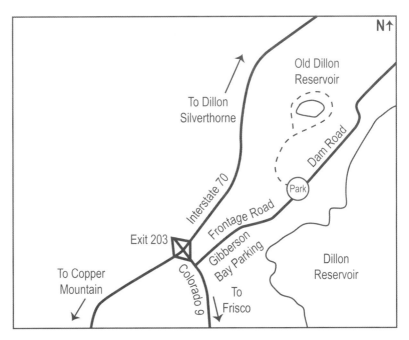

2 Sugarloaf Mountain

Sugarloaf Peak from Betasso Preserve parking area

Hike Distance: 0.6 mile each way

Hiking Time: Up in 20 minutes. Down in 18 minutes.

Starting Elevation: 8,438 feet

Highest Elevation: 8,917 feet

Elevation Gain: 479 feet

Trail: All the way

Relevant Maps: Trails Illustrated 102

    Gold Hill 7½ minute

    Boulder County

    Roosevelt National Forest

Views From the Summit: NNW to Twin Sisters Peaks

    NW to Longs Peak and Mount Meeker

    E to Boulder

    ESE to Green Mountain

    SSW to James Peak

    SE to Bear Peak and South Boulder Peak

    WNW to Paiute Peak and Mount Audubon

    WSW to Bald Mountain, South and North Arapaho Peaks

ere is an easy, early or late-season hike that is close to Boulder. A short, winding, rough road leads to an open, flat summit with great views. A fire lookout has been removed from the high point. There are several Sugarloaf Mountains in Colorado.

Getting There: From Broadway in Central Boulder, drive west on CO 119 for 5.2 miles and turn sharply right onto Sugarloaf Road. Follow Sugarloaf Road for 4.6 miles from CO 119 and turn right onto Sugarloaf Mountain Road for 0.9 mile and park in a clearing as two roads lead to the left.

The Hike: Begin up a blocked, rocky road to the north-northeast. After 75 yards, take either of two ascending routes that quickly reconnect. Follow the road as it curls toward the mountaintop. Around halfway, a sign with regulations is passed on the left. There are a few trees on the flat summit. But the vistas, especially of the Indian Peaks, are excellent. It is best to return by the road you ascended.

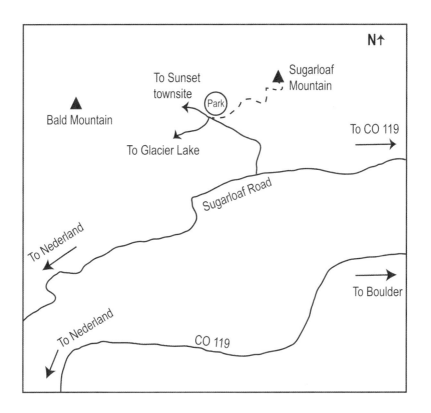

3 Mount Cutler

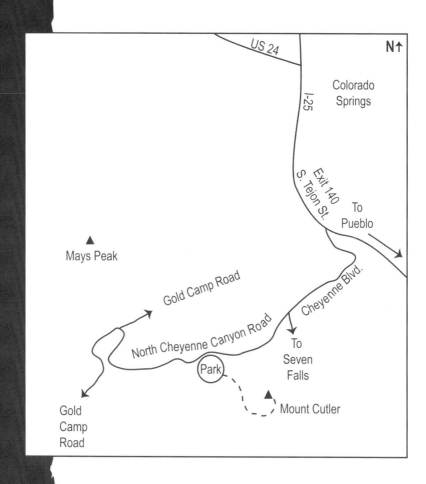

This mountain, located within North Cheyenne Cañon Park, is named after Henry Cutler, a philanthropist who gave generously to Colorado College, among others. Other trails, waterfalls, and picnic areas can be found within this Colorado Springs park. This short hike is ideal for families and, due to its low elevation, is hikeable from April through November. Bicycles and horses are forbidden on the trail, and dogs must be kept on a leash.

Getting There: From the southern part of Colorado Springs, drive south from I-25 on South Tejon Street for 0.4 mile. Then turn right on Cheyenne Boulevard and proceed southwest for 2.5 miles to an intersection with Evans Avenue, the entrance to Seven Falls (a fee area) and a sign to mark the beginning of North Cheyenne Canyon Road on the right for 1.5 more miles to a parking area and a trail sign on the left. Park here.

The Hike: Follow the clear trail up to the east-southeast as it curves to the unmarked, tree-covered top of Mount Cutler. En route to the top, there are good overlooks of Seven Falls to the south. At the high point, Mays Peak can be seen to the west-northwest, Almagre Mountain to the west, and Cheyenne Mountain to the south-southeast. The return is short and easy. It follows the ascent route.

Hike Distance: 0.75 mile each way

Hiking Time: Up in 26 minutes. Down in 21 minutes.

Starting Elevation: 6,785 feet

Highest Elevation: 7,200 feet

Elevation Gain: 485 feet (includes 35 extra feet each way)

Trail: All the way

Relevant Maps: Trails Illustrated 137

Manitou Springs 7½ minute

El Paso County Number One

Pike National Forest

North Cheyenne Cañon Park

Views From the Summit: NW to Mays Peak and North Cheyenne Cañon

E to Colorado Springs

S to Seven Falls

SE to Cheyenne Mountain

SW to St. Peter's Dome

4 St. Peter's Dome

Hike Distance: 0.8 mile each way

Hiking Time: Up in 28 minutes. Down in 21 minutes.

Starting Elevation: 9,278 feet

Highest Elevation: 9,760 feet

Elevation Gain: 612 feet (includes 65 extra feet each way)

Trail: All the way until the final 150 feet

Relevant Maps: Trails Illustrated 137

   Mount Big Chief 7½ minute

   El Paso County Number Three

   Pike National Forest

Views From the Summit: NNE to Colorado Springs

   E to Cheyenne Mountain

   S to the trailhead

   W to Mount Rosa

   WNW to Pikes Peak

St. Peter's Dome consists of two rocky peaks a hundred yards apart. The southern summit is the higher peak and the route to its top is described here. The access to the trailhead takes one over the historic Old Stage and Gold Camp Roads west of Colorado Springs. The usual season for this hike will be from April into November.

Getting There: From I-25 in southern Colorado Springs, drive south on Nevada Avenue, which becomes CO 115 for 1.8 miles, and turn right on Cheyenne Mountain Boulevard. Follow this road around a circle through various intersections for 2.4 miles to the intersection with Cheyenne Mountain Zoo Road. Continue straight on Old Stage Road for 6.8 miles and reach an intersection with Gold Camp Road. Go left for another 0.9 mile on Gold Camp Road and park on the right near a metal trail sign and a side road on the right. Regular cars can reach this point.

The Hike: From the parking area, with its great view north to Colorado Springs, hike north-northwest and follow the trail as it curves to the right and enters the trees. After a half mile from the trailhead, go left (south) at a fork. (The right fork takes you up difficult terrain to the north summit.) Follow this left fork around rocky cliffs before curving up and to the right for the final segment to the top. There is no trail for the last fifty yards. Easily ascend the rocks to a flat, unmarked summit. Enjoy the view and retrace your ascent route back to the trailhead.

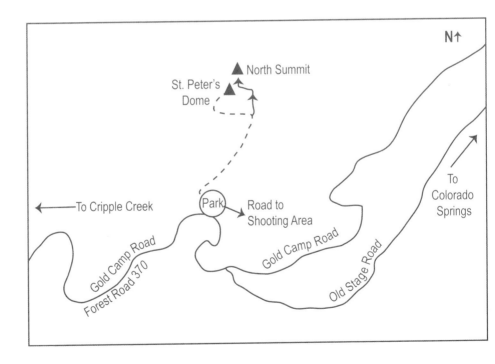

5 Smith Lake

Hike Distance: 0.75 mile each way

Hiking Time: Up in 21 minutes.
Down in 19 minutes.

Starting Elevation: 10,192 feet

Highest Elevation: 10,500 feet

Elevation Gain: 418 feet
(includes 55 extra feet each way)

Trail: All the way

Relevant Maps: Trails Illustrated 122

Orno Peak 7½ minute

Garfield County Number One

Routt National Forest

The hike to Smith Lake is short and scenic. The foliage is lush and two ponds are encountered as you ascend into the Flat Tops Wilderness. The trail is adequate and extends around this serene lake. The lake and the creek flowing from it are named after Tom Smith, a trapper, who lived in this area in the 1880s.

Getting There: From Main Street in Yampa via CO 131, take Garfield County Road 7 (which becomes Forest Road 900) and drive 16.1 miles and park on the right at the trailhead sign. (This point is 0.6 mile before the road ends at Stillwater Reservoir.)

The Hike: Start walking steeply up the trail to the northwest and soon pass an unnamed pond below on your left. Avoid a side trail on the left above this pond and stay on the main trail as it rises past another pond below on the right. Continue up and reach Smith Lake at the head of the valley. The outflow will be on your right and is easily crossed on a group of logs. A trail circles the lake and the Flat Tops can be seen above to the west-northwest. Since this hike is so short, you may wish to combine it with another in the grand Flat Tops Wilderness.

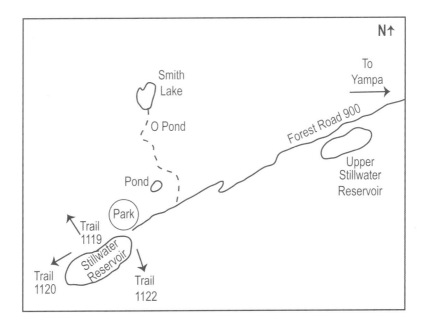

Flatirons Vista Loop

South Boulder Peak and Bear Peak from Flatirons Vista North Trail

Hike Distance: 2.6 miles (total loop)

Hiking Time: 68 minutes (total loop)

Starting Elevation: 5,920 feet

Highest Elevation: 6,080 feet

Elevation Gain: 190 feet (includes 30 extra feet)

Trail: All the way

Relevant Maps: Trails Illustrated 100

Louisville 7½ minute

Boulder County

Comprehensive Trail Map of Boulder County

Wonderful views of the Boulder Flatirons and the mountains west of Boulder are available from this broad mesa, which is maintained by the Boulder Open Space. A trail fee is required.

Getting There: Drive on CO 93 between Boulder and Golden to 0.3 mile south of the intersection with CO 128 and park in the large lot off the west side of CO 93.

The Hike: From the trailhead facilities, begin west on the Flatirons Vista South Trail. Soon pass through a gate and take a left fork. Continue west on the relatively level trail, pass the Prairie Vista Trail on the right, and quickly reach an old two-track road on the right, which is closed to bicycles. Take this road, which proceeds north amid well-spaced pine trees with great views of the Flatirons. At a T intersection, turn right and follow power poles to the east. Avoid a trail on the right and stay on the Flatirons Vista North Trail. As the trail curves right, avoid two trails on the left, which lead to the Greenbelt Plateau, and finish the loop at the trailhead.

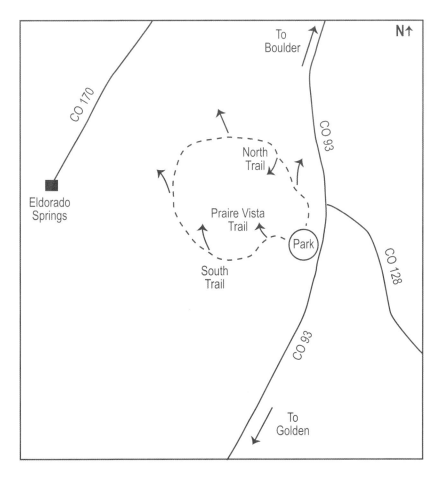

7 Bluffs Regional Park Loop

Trailhead

Hike Distance: 2.7 miles (total loop)

Hiking Time: 63 minutes (total loop)

Starting Elevation: 6,000 feet

Highest Elevation: 6,220 feet

Elevation Gain: 296 feet (includes 76 extra feet)

Trail: All the way

Relevant Maps: Highlands Ranch 7½ minute

Douglas County Number Two

Signboard at Trailhead

This park owes much to Edward E. Tepe, a Douglas County Planning Director. The loop trail is wide and well graded and passes two side trails to overlook sites, several side trails to nearby homes, and a link to the East-West Trail of Highlands Ranch. There are fine views of the Front Range from the trail. Motor vehicles are forbidden, and dogs must be on leash.

Getting There: From I-25 take Exit 193 and drive west on Lincoln Avenue about 250 yards. Then turn left on Commons Street for 2 blocks. Then turn right on Sky Ridge Avenue, cross Ridgegate Parkway and drive up Crooked Stick Trail until it ends at the parking area and trailhead at Bluffs Regional Park.

The Hike: Begin up the wide trail, and for a clockwise loop quickly continue straight and avoid the trail on the right (you will return on that trail). Ascend the Tinsley Trail and go straight at a four-way intersection at the top of the ridge. The left trail connects with the East-West Trail. The trail on the right goes to the first of two overlooks.

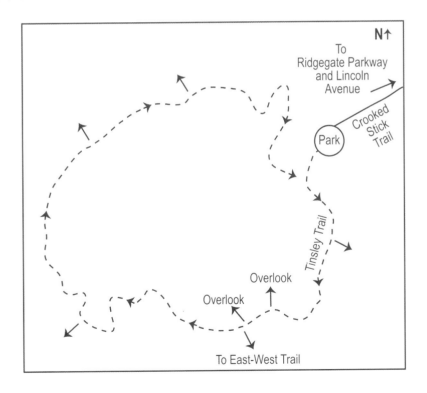

8 Panorama Point (via the Raccoon Trail)

Several trails lead to Panorama Point in Golden Gate Canyon State Park, west of Golden. This hike mostly uses the Raccoon Trail in a clockwise direction. The park offers over 60 miles of well-marked trails as well as picnic areas, camp-sites, and a visitor center. The Ken R. Larkin Memorial at Pan-orama Point features informational signs, two signboards that identify the mountains on the horizon, and an extensive deck with several overlooks.

Getting There: Drive to Golden Gate Canyon State Park by either driving west from CO 93 in Golden via Jefferson County Road 70 and CO 46 for 12.6 miles or north from U.S. 6 on CO 119 and then east on CO 46. Drive up Mountain Base Road (at the southeast quadrant of the park) for 3.1 miles to an intersection. Park around here off the road. A park fee is required.

Hike Distance: 2.5 miles (total loop)

Hiking Time: Up in 55 minutes. Down in 25 minutes (clockwise loop).

Starting Elevation: 9,160 feet

Highest Elevation: 9,320 feet

Elevation Gain: 640 feet (includes 480 extra feet)

Trail: All the way

Relevant Maps: Trails Illustrated 100

Golden Gate Canyon State Park (available at visitor center)

Black Hawk 7½ minute

Tungsten 7½ minute

Gilpin County

The Hike: Start north on the Elk Trail, which is twenty yards to the left of Mountain Base Road. Descend 100 yards to an intersection and go left on the Raccoon Trail. Continue down and keep straight as a trail enters on the left from the Reverend's Ridge Campground. Quickly arrive at another intersection at the low point of this hike, make a sharp right turn and then a quick left fork, which begins rising to Panorama Point. Follow the Raccoon Trail signs. After a steep ascent, the trail curves right at a gate and reaches a juncture with the Mule Deer Trail, alongside a dirt road, before reaching Panorama Point. (Automobile access to this point is also possible.) Enjoy the extensive vistas before continuing down by trail to the northwest. You quickly reach the end of the Raccoon Trail loop and then ascend the Elk Trail back to the road and your starting point.

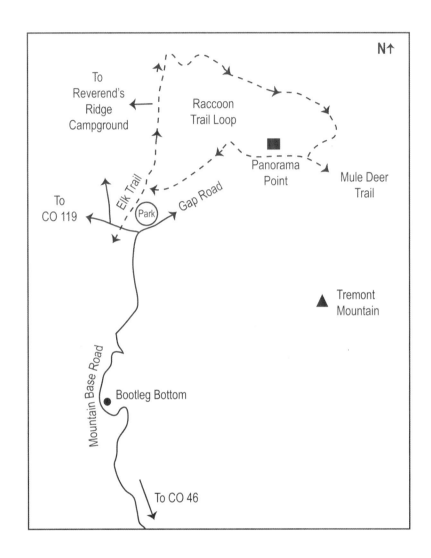

9 South Rim Loop Trail

Located southwest of Denver, near Chatfield Reservoir in Douglas County, Roxborough State Park is a treasure. It makes a fine location for a late season hike before the cross-country ski season begins. A modern visitor center, well-marked trails, and splendid rock formations combine to make this a wonderful playground for all ages. Pets and bicycles are not allowed in the park. The many picturesque red and white rocks reminds one of the Garden of the Gods in Colorado Springs and the Colorado National Monument outside of Grand Junction.

Getting There: On Santa Fe Drive (U.S. 85) in south Denver, drive south of the C-470 interchange for 4.3 miles and turn right on Titan Road (Douglas County Road 7). Set your odometer to zero. Follow Titan Road, which curves left and becomes Rampart Range Road, for a total of 6.8 miles from Santa Fe Drive. Then turn left at a sign for Roxborough Park and then right after 60 yards and enter the park at mile 7.1. An entrance fee is required. Continue on the good road and park at the trailhead on the left at mile 8.7.

The Hike: For a clockwise trip on the South Rim Loop Trail, start walking down and east-southeast from the parking area. Quickly cross a bridge and ascend to a signed fork, which is the beginning of the loop. Take the left (southeast) fork and proceed through open terrain, up a few switchbacks to reach the high point of this outing on the ridge. The view back down to the park is special. After passing a short segment of fencing, you will reach a fork. A pleasant view of the vast south Denver valley lies before you. Continue on the right (south) fork and descend through the trees for the second half of your loop. Pass an occasional bench alongside the trail and some good rocky projections and cliffs. Cross a meadow before going over a bridge and taking the first of three quick right forks. The last of these three leads to the east-southeast on the Willow Creek Trail and back to the original intersection with the South Rim Trail. Go left here and retrace your way over the first bridge and back up to your vehicle at the trailhead.

Hike Distance: 2.6 miles (total loop)

Hiking Time: 64 minutes (total loop)

Starting Elevation: 6,105 feet

Highest Elevation: 6,400 feet

Elevation Gain: 480 feet (includes 185 total extra feet)

Trail: All the way

Relevant Maps: Trails Illustrated 135

   Kassler 7½ minute

   Douglas County Number One

   Roxborough State Park

   Pike National Forest

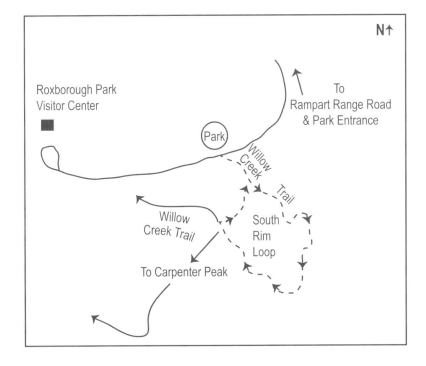

10 Green Mountain (Boulder County)

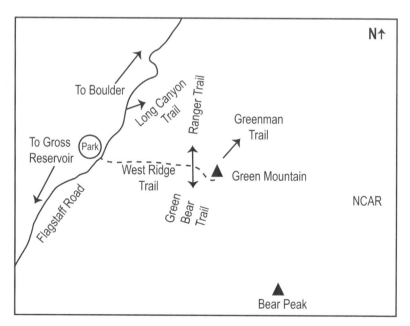

Green Mountain overlooks Boulder from the west. The route up the west ridge described here is the easiest ascent. The parks of the Boulder Open Space are exceptional in their maintenance and variety.

Getting There: From Broadway and Baseline Road in Boulder, drive west up Baseline (which becomes Flagstaff Mountain Road) for 6.1 miles to a sign and the trailhead on the left (east) at a high point of this paved road and at the Boulder Mountain Park boundary. Park around here off the road.

The Hike: Begin southeast on the clearly marked Green Mountain West Ridge Trail. The trail descends and rises on occasion as you ascend the west ridge and steepens near the top. At about two-thirds of the way up, keep straight at a four-way trail intersection. The summit lies amid large boulders and is marked by a stone column with a metal plate stating the directions and elevations of 24 visible peaks. A register cylinder lies within the column. You can descend to the north if you do not need to return to your car at the trailhead. Otherwise, descend to the south and retrace your ascent route.

Hike Distance: 1.3 miles each way

Hiking Time: Up in 40 minutes. Down in 36 minutes.

Starting Elevation: 7,690 feet

Highest Elevation: 8,144

Elevation Gain: 714 feet (includes 130 extra feet each way)

Trail: All the way

Relevant Maps: Trails Illustrated 100

Eldorado Springs 7½ minute

Boulder County

Boulder Mountain Park Trail Map

Views From the Summit: NE to Boulder

NW to McHenrys Peak, Chiefs Head Peak, Pagoda Mountain, Longs Peak, Mount Meeker, Estes Cone, Ypsilon Mountain, and Twin Sisters Peaks.

SE to Bear Peak and South Boulder Pea

SW to Thorodin Mountain, Mount Bancroft, James Peak, Mount Neva, and South Arapaho Peak

W to Indian Peaks

WNW to Bald Mountain

11   Carson Lake

Here is an easy lake hike in the wonderful Grand Mesa National Forest. Of the many lakes, some, like Carson Lake, are man-made reservoirs. The hike begins at a high point and descends through forest and meadows to reach Carson Lake, which is popular with fishing enthusiasts. A western approach from Lands End Road allows cars within 100 yards of the lake's outlet.

Getting There: From CO 65 on top of Grand Mesa near Cedaredge, drive west from the main visitor center and Road 121 for 4.6 miles and turn left (southwest) onto Lands End Road (Road 100). Follow Lands End Road for 1.3 miles and take Road 109 (the Flowing Park Road) on the left. Continue straight on Road 109 after 1.1 miles, and at mile 2.8 turn right onto Road 1B. Park after 0.3 mile as the road ends at private property and the trailhead.

The Hike: Begin southwest on Trail 728. Poles mark the trail as it descends gently through an open meadow and enters the forest. Pass under, over, or around a fence to block livestock and continue downward to a small creek crossing and across a lush meadow. Soon Carson Lake comes into view below. As the clear trail approaches the lake, take a right fork to reach a pole marker and then go left to reach the dam at Carson Lake. Your return is the more difficult part of the hike.

Hike Distance: 1.4 miles each way

Hiking Time: Out in 30 minutes. Back in 36 minutes.

Starting Elevation: 10,280 feet

Highest Elevation: 10,280 feet

Elevation Gain: 560 feet (includes 85 extra feet each way)

Trail: All the way

Relevant Maps: Trails Illustrated 136

    Hells Kitchen 7½ minute

    Mesa County Number Three

    Grand Mesa National Forest

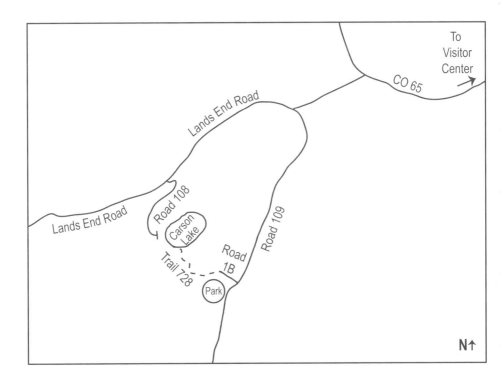

12 Farris Creek Trail

"The Cave"

Hike Distance: 1.3 miles each way

Hiking Time: Up in 44 minutes. Down in 27 minutes.

Starting Elevation: 8,760 feet

Highest Elevation: 9,700 feet

Elevation Gain: 940 feet

Trail: All the way

Relevant Maps: Trails Illustrated 131

   Cement Mountain 7½ minute

   Gunnison County Number Three

   Gunnison Basin Area

There are many connecting hiking and biking trails off of Cement Creek and Brush Creek Roads south of Crested Butte. This hike begins from the southern terminus of the Farris Creek Trail and continues north over to Brush Creek Road. This first segment is steep, rises into lovely open terrain past a scenic rock formation, and ends at a junction with the Walrod Gulch Cutoff Trail. In mid-July this is a great wildflower hike.

Getting There: From CO 135 between Crested Butte and Gunnison, drive east on Cement Creek Road 1.7 miles and park on the right with the trailhead sign on the left.

The Hike: Begin steeply up northwest. After a few hundred yards the trail begins a series of switchbacks. Above and to the right a striking large rock with an arch and a cave can be seen. After the trail breaks out of the trees, you pass through unspoiled mountain greenery and ascend above and left of the notable large rock and reach the signed fork with good vistas. The return from here will be quicker and easier than the unremitting ascent.

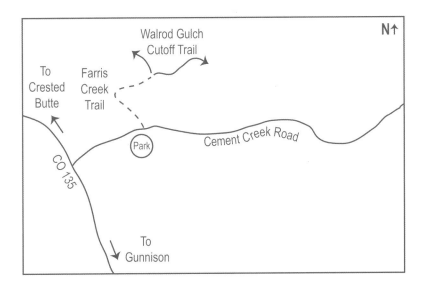

13 Coffin Lake and Little Trappers Lake

The long drive to Trappers Lake in the Flat Tops Wilderness takes you through beautiful country to an area with many hiking trails. This short hike to Coffin Lake and Little Trappers Lake begins along the left side of vast Trappers Lake and then rises through forest that was decimated by the fire of August 16, 2002, which blackened large areas of the forest in this area. The burned trees have enabled the flowers and grasses to flourish with their greater exposure to sunlight.

Hike Distance: 1.5 miles each way

Hiking Time: Up in 40 minutes. Down in 35 minutes.

Starting Elevation: 9,600 feet

Highest Elevation: 9,950 feet

Elevation Gain: 642 feet (includes 292 extra feet)

Trail: All the way

Relevant Maps: Trails Illustrated 122

Trappers Lake 7½ minute

Garfield County Number One

White River National Forest

Getting There: From the northern edge of Yampa on CO 131, drive west on Road 17, which becomes the Flat Tops Scenic Byway and changes road numbers as it crosses Dunckley Pass and Ripple Pass and connects with Meeker to the west. Drive 41.8 miles from Yampa on this road and turn left at the sign directing you to Trappers Lake. After 7.5 miles from this fork, take the road to the left and park 0.4 mile farther at the Trappers Lake Trailhead. Regular cars can reach this point.

The Hike: Begin to the south from the trailhead signboard and register. Follow the Carhart Trail, which will encircle Trappers Lake for the next five miles. However, after two-thirds of a mile you reach a signed fork with an old cabin and Trappers Lake below. Ascend the left (north-northeast) trail and meander through the burned forest. A quarter mile farther brings you to another fork. Coffin Lake is less than 100 yards up the left fork. Take this brief side trail to the shores of this long, narrow lake. Then return to the fork and continue the ascent to the east. The next 0.6 mile takes you over a high point to the right fork down to Little Trappers Lake. Return by retracing your route back to the trailhead.

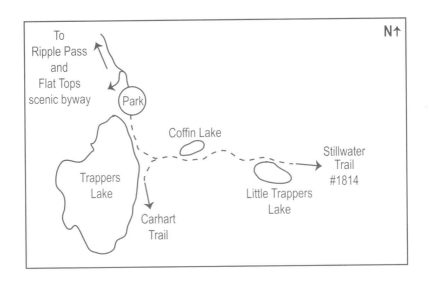

To
Ripple Pass
and
Flat Tops
scenic byway

Park

Coffin Lake

Stillwater
Trail
#1814

Trappers
Lake

Little Trappers
Lake

Carhart
Trail

Little Trappers Lake

14 City Lights Ridge

Golden Gate Canyon State Park is a hidden treasure within 30 miles of downtown Denver. The many trails are well marked. There are great picnic, camping, and fishing facilities. It is a wonderful place for families. A fee is required and pets must be kept on a leash. The side trail to City Lights Ridge is for hikers only.

Getting There: From CO 93 north of Golden, drive west on the paved Golden Gate Canyon Road for 12.7 miles to an intersection within Golden Gate Canyon State Park. An entrance fee is required and can be paid at the visitor center on the right. From the intersection, take the right fork onto Gilpin County Road 57 for 2.3 miles and park on the left near the Bridge Creek Trailhead.

The Hike: Start out northeast and cross a bridge and follow the Burro Trail. After 0.7 mile take two consecutive left forks on the Mountain Lion Trail. After 0.2 mile from the last fork, reach the trail to City Lights Ridge on the left and ascend it 0.5 mile, with occasional steep spots, past a rocky buttress on the right to the summit. Enjoy the views before retracing your route back to the trailhead.

View toward Starr Peak from City Lights Ridge

Hike Distance: 1.4 miles each way

Hiking Time: Up in 42 minutes. Down in 30 minutes.

Starting Elevation: 7,860 feet

Highest Elevation: 8,690 feet

Elevation Gain: 890 feet (includes 30 extra feet each way)

Trail: All the way

Relevant Maps: Trails Illustrated 100

Black Hawk 7½ minute

Jefferson County Number One

Roosevelt National Forest

Golden Gate Canyon State Park (available at visitor center)

Views From the Summit: NW to Starr Peak

SSW to Mount Audubon

SE to Centralia Mountain

SW to Mount Evans

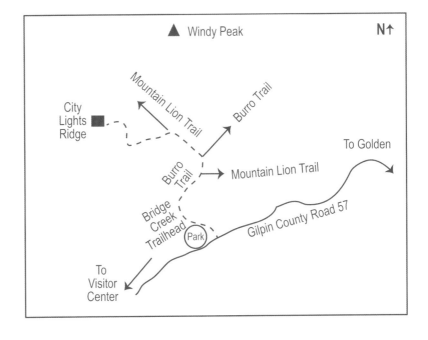

15 Mad Creek Guard Station

Hike Distance: 1.7 miles each way

Hiking Time: Up in 45 minutes. Down in 35 minutes.

Starting Elevation: 6,763 feet

Highest Elevation: 7,170 feet

Elevation Gain: 427 feet (includes 10 extra feet each way)

Trail: All the way

Relevant Maps: Trails Illustrated 117

Mad Creek 7½ minute

Rocky Peak 7½ minute

Routt County Number Four

Routt National Forest

The Mad Creek Guard Station, consisting of two old buildings in a lovely meadow, makes a fine, easy hiking destination northwest of Steamboat Springs. The gradual ascent on the Swamp Park Trail parallels the rushing waters of Mad Creek below. There are several connecting trails that offer other hiking choices. Bikes may be encountered, but motorized vehicles are forbidden on the trail. Try this one in the second half of May or in October. In the late season, however, the creek flow will be less impressive.

Getting There: From U.S. 40 (Lincoln Avenue) at the west end of Steamboat Springs, turn onto Elk River Road, which proceeds northwest to Clark and becomes Routt County Road 129. After 5.4 miles from U.S. 40, park on the right at the Mad Creek Trailhead.

The Hike: From the trailhead signs, begin northeast up the valley on the Swamp Park Trail, with Mad Creek on your right. After 1.5 miles, pass through an open gate and reach the Mad Creek Guard Station with its two wooden buildings in a large, open meadow. The trail continues up to the Mount Zirkel Wilderness and beyond. For your return, an alternative to your ascent route is to cross the meadow southeast from the Guard Station to a rough road, which crosses Mad Creek on a bridge and then meanders back to Elk River Road, a few hundred yards southeast of the Mad Creek Trailhead. This alternate descent adds an extra mile with Mad Creek out of view on your right.

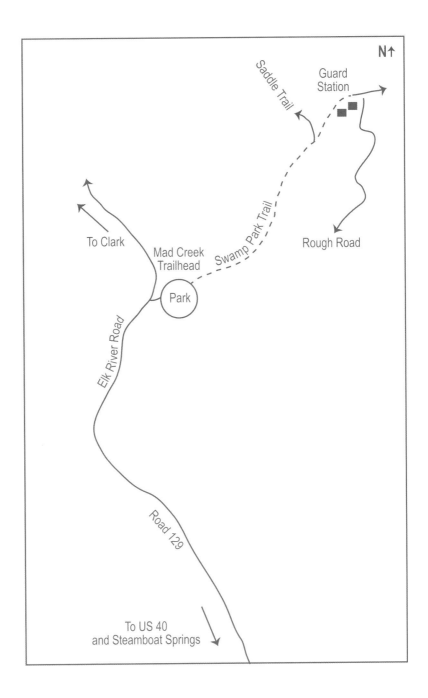

16 Devil's Head

Devils's Head Fire Lookout

The northern terminus of Rampart Range Road usually opens to automobile traffic in late May and stays open until the snows of the late fall make vehicular travel difficult. A fine hike from this road leads steeply to the Devil's Head Fire Lookout. This excellent National Recreational Trail honors Helen Dowe, the nation's first female fire lookout who worked on top of Devil's Head from 1919 to 1921. Informational signs, benches, and picnic tables occur along the trail. Dogs must be kept on a leash and motorized vehicles are prohibited. An extra bonus is a side trail near the top that leads 0.25 mile to an overlook and memorial honoring Commander Ralph Theodore Zinn, established by his wife, Edith.

Getting There: From Sedalia on U.S. 85 (south of Denver and west of Castle Rock) drive west on CO 67 for 10.1 miles to a four-way intersection. Turn left (south) onto a good, dirt road, Rampart Range Road. Stay on this main road for 8.9 miles to a fork and a sign. (The right fork continues 31 miles to Woodland Park.) Take the left fork toward the Devil's Head Campground. Keep right at two forks and after 0.5 mile from Rampart Range Road, park at a cemented area and the trailhead.

The Hike: Start the hike up stone steps to the south and pass several signs. Ascend through the forest, which includes many aspen trees and lovely rock formations. After 1.2 miles, go right at a sign, as the side trail to the Zinn Memorial Overlook leads to the left. Pass through a narrow channel between boulders and by a private cabin on the left at a small clearing and informational signs at the foot of the metal stairs, which lead to the fire lookout. One sign states the important safety rules on this final ascent. Then climb the stairs, be careful, and hopefully have a clear viewing from the porch around the lookout station. Stay on the established route and use the handrails.

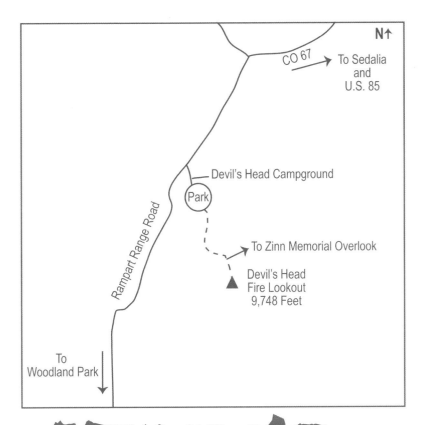

Hike Distance: 1.4 miles each way

Hiking Time: Up in 45 minutes.
Down in 30 minutes.

Starting Elevation: 8,800 feet

Highest Elevation: 9,748 feet

Elevation Gain: 1,028 feet
(includes 40 extra feet each way)

Trail: All the way

Relevant Maps: Trails Illustrated 135

Devil's Head 7½ minute

Douglas County Number One

Pike National Forest

Views From the Summit: N to Denver

NW to Mount Evans and Long Scraggy Peak

SSE to Pikes Peak

SSW to Thunder Butte

SW to Cheesman Mountain

Mount Herman

Hike Distance: 1.5 miles each way

Hiking Time: Up in 42 minutes. Down in 29 minutes.

Starting Elevation: 8,150 feet

Highest Elevation: 9,063 feet

Elevation Gain: 995 feet (includes 41 extra feet each way)

Trail: All the way

Relevant Maps: Trails Illustrated 137

Palmer Lake 7½ minute

El Paso County Number One

Pike National Forest

Views From the Summit: NNW to Mount Evans

NW to Long Scraggy Peak

SSE to Air Force Academy and Colorado Springs

SSW to Pikes Peak

E to Monument Rock and Monument Lake

This short, steep outing rises to a flat summit over a gravel trail and provides good vistas.

Getting There: From CO 105 in Monument, drive west on Second Street 0.7 mile and turn left on Mitchell Avenue for 0.6 mile. Then turn right on Mount Herman Road. It is 5.0 miles on this road to the trailhead (Trail 716) on the right.

The Hike: Begin east on Trail 716 and ascend the good main trail. Avoid occasional side trails as the main trail arrives at a sharp right turn. Rise through some steep segments and be careful with your footing on the gravel. Cairns mark the upper half of the trail. When you arrive at a point just below the ridge, the trail turns left (north) and curves right just before reaching the level high point. A pole with a banner and a register indicate the summit. A windsock lies below on the right. Enjoy the view before the more rapid return.

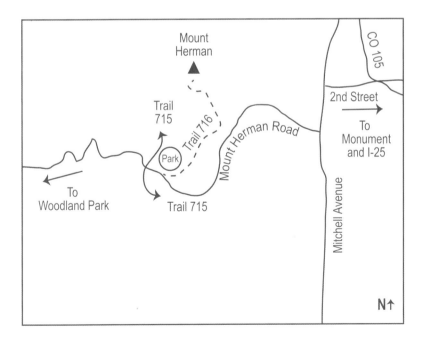

18 Devil's Backbone Park—Keyhole to the Hunter Loop

Devil's Backbone

Hike Distance: 1.8 miles each way

Hiking Time: Out in 47 minutes. Back in 38 minutes.

Starting Elevation: 5,350 feet

Highest Elevation: 5,550 feet

Elevation Gain: 390 feet (includes 190 extra feet)

Trail: All the way

Relevant Maps: Devil's Backbone Open Space (available at trailhead)

Masonville 7½ minute

Larimer County Number Four

This trail runs north all the way to Horsetooth Reservoir. Several loop trails occur along this trail. Due to usually mild winters, this collection of trails can be hiked most of the year.

Getting There: From the junction with U.S. 287 in central Loveland, drive 3.4 miles west on U.S. 34 and at a sign turn right toward Devil's Backbone Open Space and after 0.4 mile, park at the trailhead.

The Hike: Begin to the east and descend briefly and proceed northwest with the rocky projections, known as the Devil's Backbone, on the left. After 0.4 mile, keep left at a fork onto a hiker-only trail. Another 0.8 mile reaches a fork with a rocky keyhole above on the left and a bypass trail on the right. Continue north on either trail. Both trails reconnect and lead up through red cliffs to reach signs at the beginning of the Hunter Loop and an overlook north. This is the turnaround point of this hike. On the return, keep left at the first encountered fork.

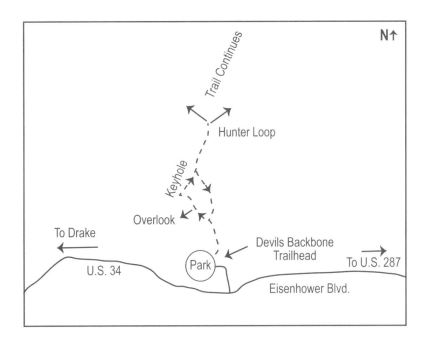

19 | South Valley Park Loop

R ed rock formations dot the landscape and make South Valley a special park. Signs offer information along this trail loop. No fee is required in this Jefferson County park. Rock climbing is prohibited.

Getting There: From C-470 drive south on South Wadsworth Boulevard (CO 121) for 200 yards and turn right onto Deer Creek Canyon Road. Stay on this road 3.1 miles to the west and park on the right near the trailhead.

The Hike: Start out up to the northeast on the wide Coyote Song Trail. At a trail crest descend to a fork. Continue left on the hikers-only Swallow Trail. Pass a pond on the left and reach a four-way intersection at mile 1.5 of this hike. Take the left fork toward the road, which you will cross, and reach the Valley View Trail. After 1.2 miles on this trail, cross the road and within 100 yards join the Swallow Trail on the left. Ascend and complete the loop via the Coyote Song Trail back to the trailhead.

Hike Distance: 3.7 miles (total loop)

Hiking Time: 80 minutes (total loop)

Starting Elevation: 5,840 feet

Highest Elevation: 6,000 feet

Elevation Gain: 380 feet (includes 220 extra feet)

Trail: All the way

Relevant Maps: Trails Illustrated 100

   Indian Hills 7½ minute

   Jefferson County Number Two

   South Valley Park (available at trailhead)

Coyote Song Trail

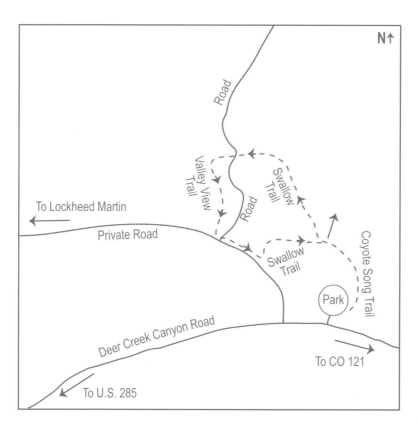

N↑

Road

Valley View Trail

Swallow Trail

Road

To Lockheed Martin

Private Road

Swallow Trail

Coyote Song Trail

Park

Deer Creek Canyon Road

To CO 121

To U.S. 285

20 Maroon Lake to Crater Lake

Maroon Lake and the Maroon Bells

With the massive Maroon Bells above, this is a very scenic hike and a very popular area, especially with the turning of the aspen from green to yellow and red in the middle of September.

Getting There: From CO 82 in Aspen at a roundabout, drive up Maroon Creek Road for 9 miles and park as the road ends. A fee is required. At certain times car traffic is forbidden and the visitor is required to take a bus to the trailhead.

The Hike: Begin on the trail along the right side of Maroon Lake. At signs, take the trail on the right and ascend the valley with Maroon Creek on the left. Follow the trail as it rises steeply at intervals. Ascend some switchbacks before passing through a talus field. Soon pass a cairn and a trail ascending on the left. (This trail leads to Pyramid Peak, a fourteener.) Continue straight to the highest point of this hike. Crater Lake will be visible ahead. Continue down to a signed fork and go left to reach Crater Lake. (The right fork leads to Buckskin Pass and Willow Lake.) The Maroon Bells loom awesomely above south-southwest. Pyramid Peak is southeast and Sievers Mountain is the rocky ridge above to the north-northwest. Return by your ascent route. (The trail continues south from Crater Lake to West Maroon Pass and beyond.)

Hike Distance: 1.8 miles each way

Hiking Time: Up in 51 minutes. Back in 46 minutes.

Starting Elevation: 9,580 feet

Highest Elevation: 10,159 feet

Elevation Gain: 798 feet (includes 219 extra feet)

Trail: All the way

Relevant Maps: Trails Illustrated 128

Maroon Bells 7½ minute

Pitkin County Number One

White River National Forest

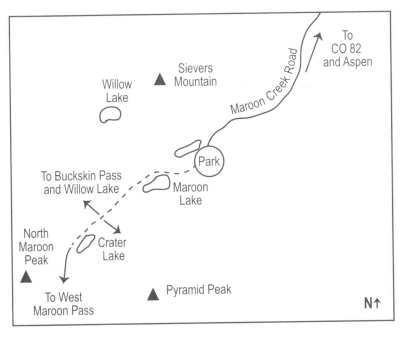

21 Monarch Lake Loop

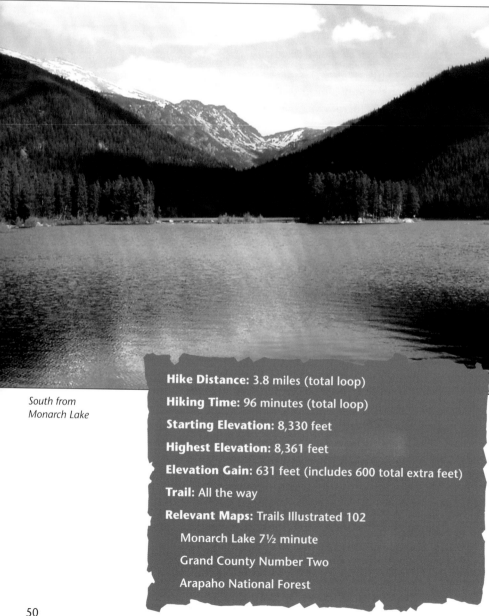

South from Monarch Lake

Hike Distance: 3.8 miles (total loop)

Hiking Time: 96 minutes (total loop)

Starting Elevation: 8,330 feet

Highest Elevation: 8,361 feet

Elevation Gain: 631 feet (includes 600 total extra feet)

Trail: All the way

Relevant Maps: Trails Illustrated 102

Monarch Lake 7½ minute

Grand County Number Two

Arapaho National Forest

With picnic tables, toilets, and informational signs near the trailhead, the loop around Monarch Lake provides an easy, refreshing hike in the beautiful Indian Peaks Wilderness. Bikes are forbidden and dogs must be kept on a leash. This trek begins at a confluence of trails. The Cascade Trail goes to the left and the Southside Trail, which is part of the Continental Divide Trail, proceeds to the right over the dam, and connects eventually with both the High Lonesome Trail and the Cascade Trail.

Getting There: From U.S. 40 at the western edge of Granby, drive north on U.S. 34 for 5.4 miles. Then turn right on Arapaho Bay Road (Grand County Number 6), and drive on the good main road for another 9.5 miles to a road barrier at Monarch Lake. Park nearby.

The Hike: For a clockwise loop around the lake, begin east-southeast on the left fork at the big trail sign at the lake. Follow this Cascade Creek Trail alongside the lake, pass the wilderness boundary, and then enter the woods with the creek on your right until you reach a signed fork. Go to the right (southwest) on the Southside Trail. Soon cross Buchanan Creek and 0.6 mile farther cross Arapaho creek, both on sturdy bridges. Within 0.25 mile, pass the High Lonesome Trail and a cabin ruin on the left and continue straight ahead (west). Before long, leave the wilderness area and pass a large, old, abandoned engine. Continue through the thin forest with Monarch Lake on your right. The trail becomes less defined here but can still be followed. Pass between two large log bins before curving around the edge of the lake to the dam and the end of the loop and your vehicle 100 yards to the left.

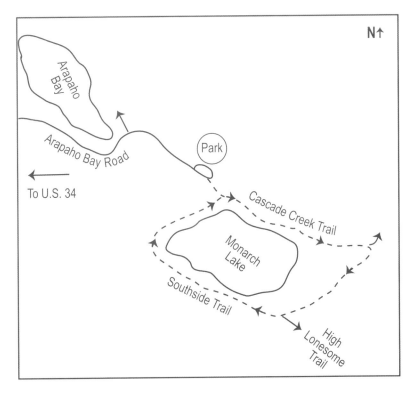

22 Pumphouse Lake and Corona Lake

Corona Lake

Hike Distance: 1.0 mile each way

Hiking Time: Out in 25 minutes. Back in 21 minutes.

Starting Elevation: 11,600 feet

Highest Elevation: 11,600 feet

Lowest Elevation: 11,206 feet

Elevation Gain: 544 feet (includes 75 extra feet each way)

Trail: All the way

Relevant Maps: Trails Illustrated 103

    East Portal 7½ minute

    Grand County Number Four

    Arapaho National Forest

The Rollins Pass road provides access to grassy slopes and great vistas below the Continental Divide. Pumphouse Lake lies at the foot of Mount Epworth. The trail continues down to prettier Corona Lake and the end of the trail. Corona was a settlement near Rollins Pass.

Getting There: From U.S. 40 at the southern edge of Winter Park, access Rollins Pass road and set your mileage to zero. Drive up this unpaved road for 12.9 miles and park off-road with the trailhead on the left. En route to this trailhead, keep straight on Road 149 at mile 3.7 and again at mile 6.4. Regular cars with good clearance can reach this trailhead.

The Hike: Start down an old rough road to the north-northwest. Within 100 yards take a left fork and leave the road. Soon pass Pumphouse Lake about 50 yards on the left. Two side trails descend to the lake. Cross the outflow from Pumphouse Lake and quickly take a right fork and cross the creek again. (The left fork descends west along Ranch Creek.) The trail then reaches an overlook of Corona Lake and leads down to it.

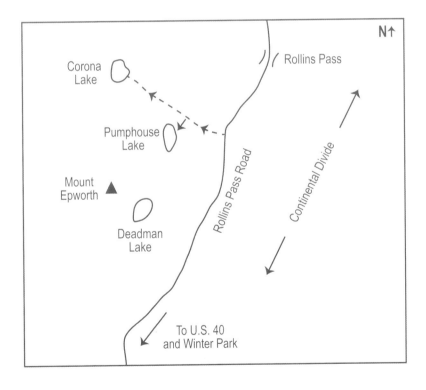

23 Nymph Lake, Dream Lake, and Emerald Lake

T his hike to three small, beautiful lakes in Rocky Mountain National Park begins at Bear Lake, one of the most popular areas within the park. To encounter less hiker traffic, try this one mid-week. The short length and modest elevation gain make this outing ideal for families. Other trails connect Bear Lake with Bierstadt Lake, Glacier Gorge Junction, Flattop Mountain, and Fern Lake. The usually crowded Bear Lake parking area has an information booth, a shuttle-bus stop, and toilet facilities.

Getting There: At the western edge of Estes Park, enter Rocky Mountain National Park at the Beaver Meadows Entrance. A fee is required and no pets are allowed on the trails. Drive west 0.2 mile from this entrance and turn left onto Bear Lake Road. Follow this road for 9 more miles to road end at the Bear Lake parking area.

The Hike: Begin on foot from the upper edge of the parking area and take the trail on the left at a sign. Within 30 yards, take a right fork and ascend 0.5 mile to small, serene Nymph Lake. Water lilies often cover part of the lake. Longs Peak, Pagoda Mountain, and Thatchtop Mountain can be seen to the southeast over the lake. Continue west on the excellent trail another 0.6 mile to Dream Lake, which is the longest of these three lakes. Just before reaching Dream Lake, avoid the left trail to Lake Haiyaha. Follow the right fork along the northern edge of Dream Lake and up 0.7 mile to trail's end at the rocky bowl of Emerald Lake. The trail becomes more rocky and steep just before this final lake. Tyndall Gorge and Hallett Peak hover above to the southwest. Savor the beauty and the easy return to Bear Lake.

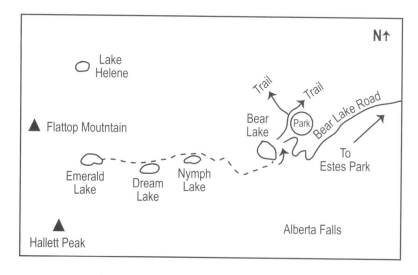

Emerald Lake and Hallett Peak

Hike Distance: 0.5 mile to Nymph Lake; 0.6 mile to Dream Lake; 0.7 mile to Emerald Lake. (Total 1.8 miles each way)

Hiking Time: Up in 42 minutes. Down in 38 minutes.

Starting Elevation: 9,475 feet

Highest Elevation: 10,140 feet

Elevation Gain: 970 feet (includes 305 extra feet)

Trail: All the way

Relevant Maps: Trails Illustrated 200 or 301

McHenry's Peak 7½ minute

Larimer County Number Three

Rocky Mountain National Park

24 Hanging Lake

This is a very popular hike for tourists and families. There are occasional benches along the trail and seven bridges cross Dead Horse Creek on your way to this different and scenic lake with Bridal Veil Falls and Spouting Rock above. Dogs are forbidden.

Getting There: From I-70 east of Glenwood Springs from the east, take Exit 121 and return east to Exit 125, which leads into a large parking area. If driving from the west, take Exit 125 as well.

The Hike: From the parking area, begin north-northeast past the visitor center to the trailhead where you ascend left (north). A steep rocky trail leads to the first of seven bridges over Dead Horse Creek. In the early season, the rushing water on this hike can be special. Pass a right fork, the Dead Horse Trail, and later a small shelter on the left. Curve right onto a trail with a metal railing on the right before reaching a side trail on the left to Spouting Rock, a worthwhile brief side trip. Continue straight over a wooden walkway at this scenic lake with Bridal Veil Falls and Spouting Rock feeding it from above. Return more quickly by your ascent route.

Hike Distance: 1.8 miles each way

Hiking Time: Up in 47 minutes. Down in 36 minutes.

Starting Elevation: 6,120 feet

Highest Elevation: 7,170 feet

Elevation Gain: 1,070 feet (includes 10 extra feet each way)

Trail: All the way

Relevant Maps: Trails Illustrated 123

Shoshone 7½ minute

Garfield County Number Five

White River National Forest

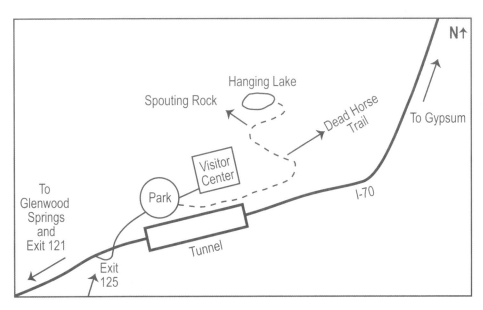

N↑

Hanging Lake

Spouting Rock

Dead Horse Trail

To Gypsum

Visitor Center

Park

To Glenwood Springs and Exit 121

I-70

Tunnel

Exit 125

25 Kruger Rock

Hermit Park is named after a solitary drifter who lived in a small cabin in the area. This county park has many amenities and, in addition to this trail, has a longer trail that leads to Homestead Meadows.

Getting There: From Lyons, take U.S. 36 northwest for 16.4 miles and turn left into Hermit Park at the sign. Register and pay an entry fee at the park office and continue up the good dirt road for 2.4 miles and go left at a fork and park in the lot on the right after 100 yards.

The Hike: Begin west on a trail, which begins at a signboard. Pass through a picnic area toward a stop sign and a road. Cross the road and begin the Kruger Rock Trail at a sign. (The trail data begins at this point.) Follow the good trail with many switchbacks as it curls up to the base of Kruger Rock. Ascend a rocky channel with some easy hand work 25 yards to the flat summit. Enjoy the great views.

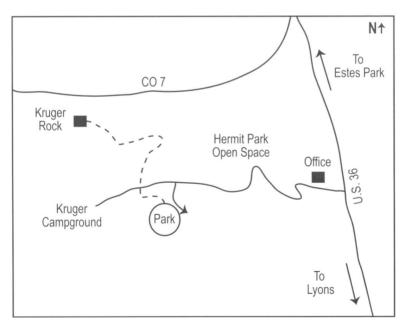

Group at Kruger Rock

Hike Distance: 1.8 miles each way

Hiking Time: Up in 60 minutes. Down in 43 minutes.

Starting Elevation: 8,320 feet

Highest Elevation: 9,355 feet

Elevation Gain: 1,279 feet (includes 122 extra feet each way)

Trail: All the way

Relevant Maps: Trails Illustrated 101

Panorama Peak 7½ minute

Larimer County Number Four

Roosevelt National Forest

Hermit Park Open Space (available at park office)

Views From the Summit: NNW to Lake Estes

SW to Mount Meeker and Longs Peak

WNW to Deer Mountain

WSW to Flattop Mountain

26 Arthurs Rock

Hike Distance: 1.8 miles each way

Hiking Time: Up in 55 minutes. Down in 42 minutes.

Starting Elevation: 5,620 feet

Highest Elevation: 6,780 feet

Elevation Gain: 1,320 feet (includes 80 extra feet each way)

Trail: All the way

Relevant Maps: Horsetooth Reservoir 7½ minute

Lory State Park

Larimer County Number Four

Roosevelt National Forest

Views From the Summit: NE to SE to Horsetooth Reservoir

E to Fort Collins

S to Horsetooth Rock

With extensive facilities, miles of good hiking trails, and a new visitor center, Lory State Park, northwest of Fort Collins, is a good destination for families who enjoy the outdoors. Due to the modest elevations at its highest points, the park offers especially good hiking for the early and late hiking seasons. Horsetooth Reservoir lies nearby, east of the park. This hike uses the shorter trail to Arthurs Rock. The Timber Trail is twice as long and starts from a parking area 100 yards south of the new visitor center.

Getting There: From the stop light in the middle of LaPorte (northwest of Fort Collins), drive west on Road 54G for 1.9 miles. Then turn left onto Rist Canyon Road (Road 52E) for 0.9 mile. Then turn left onto Road 23 and follow it for 1.4 miles until you turn right on Road 25G, which leads to the Lory State Park entrance in 1.6 more miles. Enter the park and pay the entry fee at the new visitor center 0.3 mile inside the park. It is 2.2 more miles on the main road to the south and the parking area at the southern trailhead for Arthurs Rock.

The Hike: Start west, cross a small wooden bridge, bypass the West Valley Trail and the Overlook Trail on the right, and proceed up a narrow canyon. The clear and well-marked trail then ascends the valley and passes through considerable open terrain. Follow the signs at trail intersections. At mile 1.7, the Timber Trail is joined as you proceed to the right and quickly descend about 25 feet to reach a rocky chute ascending to the left. At the top of this gully, there is an overlook with the unmarked high point of Arthurs Rock 50 yards to the left past a solitary tree. Be very careful on the bare rock. Enjoy the views, if weather permits, before retracing your ascent route back to the trailhead.

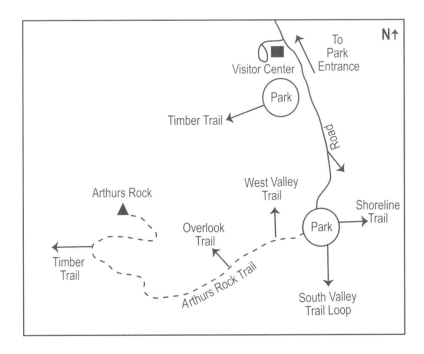

27 Clifford Griffin Memorial

F or anyone interested in the artifacts of abandoned mines, this is a special hike. A fringe benefit is experiencing the old town of Silver Plume, which most people bypass.

Getting There: From I-70 southwest of Georgetown, take Exit 226 into Silver Plume. Drive to Main Street and park near the intersection with Silver Street.

The Hike: Ascend Silver Street to the north. As the street ends, take the 730 Mine Trail at a sign on the right. Follow this trail and avoid a side trail on the left. A series of switchbacks takes you past the remnants of many old mines as you rise above Silver Plume overlooking I-70. The trail is rocky and narrow at times with steep drop-offs to the south. At a metal grate on the right and a cairn and side trail on the left, descend left 35 feet to the Clifford Griffin Memorial, a white marble spire with information about the son who died in this area over 125 years ago. Return by retracing your ascent route.

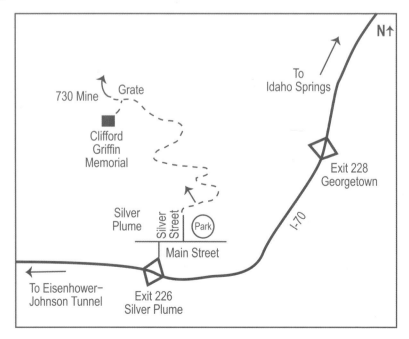

Hike Distance: 1.8 miles each way

Hiking Time: Up in 65 minutes. Down in 46 minutes.

Starting Elevation: 9,160 feet

Highest Elevation: 10,350 feet

Elevation Gain: 1,251 feet (includes 61 extra feet)

Trail: All the way

Relevant Maps: Trails Illustrated 104

    Georgetown 7½ minute

    Clear Creek County

    Arapaho National Forest

Group at Clifford Griffin Memorial

28 Frazer Meadow

Frazer Meadow can be reached from several trailheads within Golden Gate Canyon State Park. This route takes you past many aspen trees. The whole family will enjoy this outing in mid-September to see the golden, changing leaves of the aspen. A fee is required for this and all state parks. Dogs must be kept on a leash.

Getting There: Northwest of Golden from CO 93, drive west on Jefferson County Road 70, Golden Gate Canyon Road, for 12.6 miles and turn right at an intersection onto Gilpin County Road 57. The visitor center for Golden Gate Canyon State Park will be on the right. Continue 0.5 mile on Gilpin 57 and park on the left at the Frazer Meadow Trailhead.

The Hike: Start to the north from the trailhead sign. Cross the creek and continue up the gulch on the Horseshoe Trail. After 1.2 miles of walking parallel to the creek and two more creek crossings, you reach a signed fork. The trail on the right leads to Greenfield Campground. Take the left fork, soon make another creek crossing and keep straight (north-northwest) at another fork. Pass attractive rock formations on the right and keep right at another sign and trail intersection. You now enter a lovely meadow and follow the trail across the creek to reach two barn ruins in the midst of Frazer Meadow. The trail continues as the Mule Deer Trail, but this is a good turnaround point. Enjoy it all and take some refreshment before your easier return.

Hike Distance: 2.2 miles each way

Hiking Time: Up in 56 minutes. Down in 40 minutes.

Starting Elevation: 8,200 feet

Highest Elevation: 9,050 feet

Elevation Gain: 900 feet (includes 25 extra feet each way)

Trail: All the way

Relevant Maps: Trails Illustrated 100

Golden Gate Canyon State Park

Black Hawk 7½ minute

Gilpin County

Roosevelt National Forest

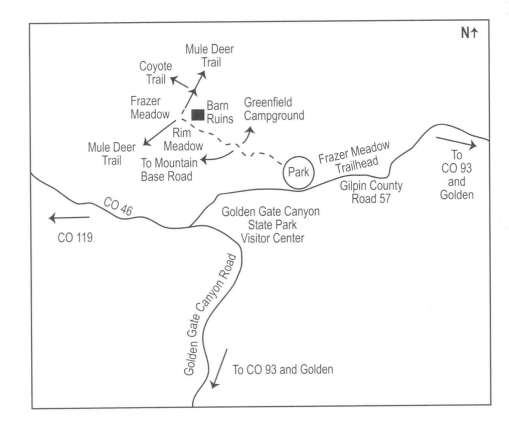

29 Mount Galbraith Loop

A good trail and proximity to Denver make this a prime hike. Another route to the summit ascends Nightbird Gulch from residential Golden.

Getting There: From CO 93 in north Golden, go west on Golden Gate Canyon Road (Jefferson County Road 70) for 1.3 miles and park in the lot down on the left.

The Hike: Proceed south from the signboard on the Cedar Gulch Trail, which winds up the canyon for 1.3 miles to reach the Loop Trail and the Nightbird Gulch Trail. For a clockwise loop, ascend left to the high point of the loop. A faint trail rises to the right and leads to the summit tree rising from rocks. Return to the loop trail and continue west. The trail curves right and completes the loop 1.3 miles from your starting point.

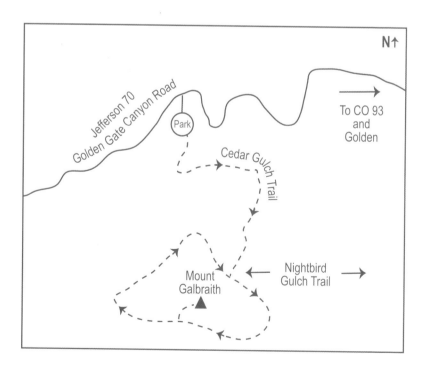

Hike Distance: 4.2 miles (total loop)

Hiking Time: Up in 75 minutes. Down in 65 minutes.

Starting Elevation: 6,240 feet

Highest Elevation: 7,240 feet

Elevation Gain: 1,240 feet (includes 240 extra feet)

Trail: All the way

Relevant Maps: Trails Illustrated 100

    Ralston Buttes 7½ minute

    Jefferson County Number One

    Mount Galbraith Park (available at Cedar Gulch Trailhead)

Views From the Summit: NE to Standley Lake and North Table Mountain

    SSE to Lookout Mountain

    SSW to Squaw Mountain

    SE to Green Mountain (Lakewood)

    SW to Mount Evans

30 Hancock Lake, Upper Hancock Lake, and Chalk Creek Pass

This short hike offers many features. There are two alpine lakes, a high mountain pass east of the Continental Divide and lots of old mining ruins en route to the trailhead. The Continental Divide Trail will be used for the hike and is part of the roads used to reach the trailhead.

Getting There: From U.S. 285, 5.4 miles south of the intersection with U.S. 24 in Buena Vista, drive west on Chaffee County Road 162 for 15.3 miles. Then take a left fork onto Hancock Road just before Saint Elmo and set your mileage to zero. Keep straight at mile 2.9 and reach the former townsite of Hancock at mile 5.3. Continue across a bridge and reach another fork at mile 5.4. It will be 1.6 more miles up the left fork to the Hancock Lake Trailhead and four-wheel drive will be required. So either walk or drive this final road segment.

The Hike: Begin south from the Hancock Lake Trailhead and quickly reach Hancock Lake on the left. Continue to the right of the lake and follow the rough trail up the valley to a signed fork. The right fork is a short trip to Upper Hancock Lake. The left fork ascends to the east-southeast and reaches Chalk Creek Pass in a few switchbacks over mostly grassy slopes. The pass is only marked by a pole in a rock pile. From the pass, you can look south down the drainage of the Middle Fork of the Arkansas River. Sewanee Peak lies above the pass to the northeast. Mount Aetna can be seen down the valley to the southeast and Van Wert Mountain is visible to the west-southwest.

Hike Distance: 1.4 miles each way to Chalk Creek Pass

Hiking Time: Up in 42 minutes. Down in 31 minutes.

Starting Elevation: 11,645 feet

Highest Elevation: 12,125 feet

Elevation Gain: 606 feet (includes 63 extra feet each way)

Trail: All the way

Relevant Maps: Trails Illustrated 130

    Garfield 7½ minute

    Chaffee County Number Three

    San Isabel National Forest

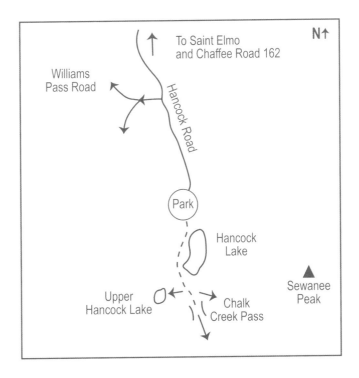

31 Long Lake and Lake Isabelle

Hike Distance: 2.0 miles each way

Hiking Time: Up in 47 minutes. Down in 38 minutes.

Starting Elevation: 10,520 feet

Highest Elevation: 10,868 feet

Elevation Gain: 508 feet (includes 80 extra feet each way)

Trail: All the way

Relevant Maps: Trails Illustrated 102

Ward 7½ minute

Boulder County

Roosevelt National Forest

Lake Isabelle and Shoshoni Peak

The Indian Peaks Wilderness is very popular for two main reasons. The scenery is gorgeous, and the area is easily reached from Boulder and Denver. The usual hiking season here is from mid-July through October. This easy hike to Long Lake and Lake Isabelle brings you up a lovely valley along South Saint Vrain Creek with several of the Indian Peaks looming above to the west.

Getting There: From the town of Nederland, west of Boulder, drive northwest on CO 72 for 11.8 miles and turn left onto Brainard Lake Road. After 2.6 miles, pass a fee station and continue 3.1 more miles and park at the Long Lake Trailhead. En route to this parking area, keep right at mile 4.7 and left at mile 4.8 (from CO 72). Drive along the right side of Brainard Lake, then turn right at mile 5.3 and left at mile 5.4. The parking area fills up early, therefore get there very early.

The Hike: Begin on the good trail to the southwest. After a few hundred yards keep right as the Jean Lunning Trail goes to the left and encircles Long Lake. Continue southwest with Long Lake on your left. After 1 mile from the trailhead go right at a signed fork and ascend the valley another mile to beautiful Lake Isabelle. At the initial part of the lake, the Pawnee Pass Trail ascends to the right.

Enjoy the grandeur of Lake Isabelle with conical Navajo Peak and Apache Peak to the southwest and the dramatic, jagged summit of Shoshoni Peak to the west-southwest. The trail continues up the basin to Isabelle Glacier. For variety on your return, you may take the Jean Lunning Trail around Long Lake in a counterclockwise direction. To do so take a sharp right at the sign and fork at the western end of Long Lake.

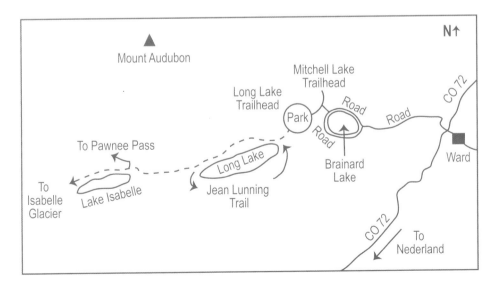

32 Cub Lake (Rocky Mountain National Park)

Hike Distance: 2.3 miles each way

Hiking Time: Up in 56 minutes. Down in 45 minutes.

Starting Elevation: 8,080 feet

Highest Elevation: 8,620 feet

Elevation Gain: 930 feet (includes 195 extra feet each way)

Trail: All the way

Relevant Maps: Trails Illustrated 200 or 301

Longs Peak 7½ minute

McHenrys Peak 7½ minute

Larimer County Number Three

Rocky Mountain National Park

Cub Lake is one of the easier hiking destinations in magnificent Rocky Mountain National Park. It's ideal for families. Due to its lower elevation and the heavy use of the trail, which packs down the snow in the early season, Cub Lake is usually hikeable at least from April through November. In the summer, water lilies cover the lake in a picturesque way. Remnants of the Fern Lake fire of 2012 are evident en route and around the lake.

Getting There: From Estes Park, enter Rocky Mountain National Park by the Beaver Meadows entrance. After 0.2 mile from the entrance station, turn left onto Bear Lake Road. After 1.3 miles on Bear Lake Road, turn right onto Moraine Park Road. Take the left fork on this road after 0.5 mile and drive another 1.1 miles and park on the left at the Cub Lake Trailhead.

The Hike: From the trailhead, begin south on the well-marked trail and cross over the Big Thompson River on a bridge. Pass along the western edge of Moraine Park and follow the trail as it curves to the right, passing a trail on the left and enter the trees. Several beaver ponds lie to the left of the trail as you proceed generally southwest with Cub Creek always on your left. Finally you emerge into an open valley with Cub Lake in its midst and the two towers of Stones Peak standing impressively to the west. Enjoy the lovely lake and friendly birds and realize how much you have to be grateful for, including this wonderful National Park. An alternate but longer way back to the trailhead involves continuing west on the trail, taking a right fork to The Pool, a lovely area of rushing water, and then back to the northeast along the Big Thompson River to the trailhead. Otherwise, return as you ascended via Moraine Park.

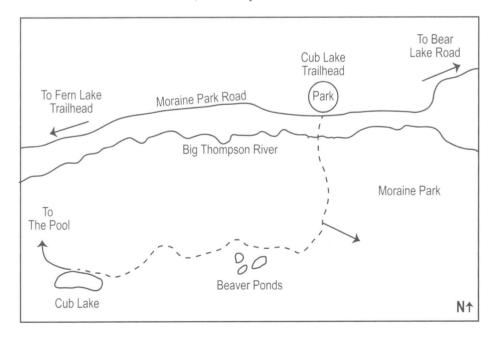

33 Chief Mountain

Chief Mountain is a good destination every month of the year. Proximity to Denver and Evergreen makes this trek a delightful half-day outing. The views from the rocky, often windblown summit reward your efforts.

Getting There: From CO 74 between Bergen Park and Evergreen, drive west on Squaw Pass Road, which becomes CO 103, for 12.2 miles and park on the right, with ski lifts below on your right.

The Hike: Cross the road and begin your ascent at a marker. A stone marker with the number 290 will be visible and is quickly passed as the trail zigzags through the trees to a four-way intersection after 0.4 mile. Continue the ascent by proceeding straight (southeast) past a Chief Mountain sign on the right. After another 0.3 mile through forest, you reach a saddle between Papoose Mountain on the left and Chief Mountain to the right. Continue up to the south for about 100 yards. The trail then curves sharply to the right (northwest). Traverse the pine forest until you reach a treeless area below the summit. Switchbacks then lead to the base of the high point. Carefully ascend the rocks and enjoy the great summit vistas before the return.

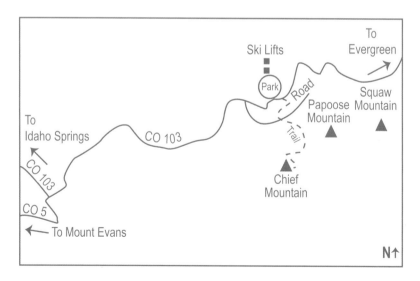

Hike Distance: 1.5 miles each way

Hiking Time: Up in 45 minutes. Down in 38 minutes.

Starting Elevation: 10,680 feet

Highest Elevation: 11,709 feet

Elevation Gain: 1,129 feet (includes 50 extra feet each way)

Trail: All the way

Relevant Maps: Trails Illustrated 104

    Idaho Springs 7½ minute

    Clear Creek County

    Arapaho National Forest

Views From the Summit: NNW to Longs Peak

    NW to James Peak

    ENE to Squaw Mountain

    SE to Pikes Peak

    SW to Mount Evans

    WSW to Grays Peak and Torreys Peak

Jackie Muller on Chief Mountain

34 Mosquito Lake

The Flat Tops Wilderness is a huge, user-friendly area for outdoor enthusiasts in north central Colorado. The beautiful landscape is less steep, and there are a large number of trails. Mosquito Lake is one of the shorter Flat Tops hikes, but there are many rewards. The trail overlooks large Stillwater Reservoir in its first part and makes three creek crossings before reaching the lake. Characteristic Flat Tops peaks lie above and, at the right time, the wildflowers can be splendid. I encountered only an average number of mosquitoes at the lake.

Getting There: From the south end of Main Street in the town of Yampa, off of CO 131, drive west on Garfield Road Number 7 for 16.7 miles and park at the end of the road at Stillwater Reservoir. This road becomes Forest Road 900 en route to the trailhead parking area.

The Hike: Begin south-southwest from the parking area, keep straight at the dam and traverse an open side slope with Stillwater Reservoir on your left. After 0.7 mile from the trailhead, take the left fork at signs and a trail register. You are now on the Bear River Trail (Number 1120). Pass through some more open meadow before entering the forest as the trail curves to the right and soon reaches Mosquito Lake in a large bowl with the Devils Causeway visible to the northwest. Many trees in the area have been defoliated by a bark beetle infestation, which is said to have occurred over 40 years ago. The trail continues on toward several possible destinations, including Trappers Lake and the Devils Causeway.

Family group at Mosquito Lake

Hike Distance: 2.2 miles each way

Hiking Time: Up in 52 minutes. Down in 50 minutes.

Starting Elevation: 10,270 feet

Highest Elevation: 10,620 feet

Elevation Gain: 780 feet (includes 215 extra feet each way)

Trail: All the way

Relevant Maps: Trails Illustrated 122

　　　Devil's Causeway 7½ minute

　　　Garfield County Number One

　　　Routt National Forest

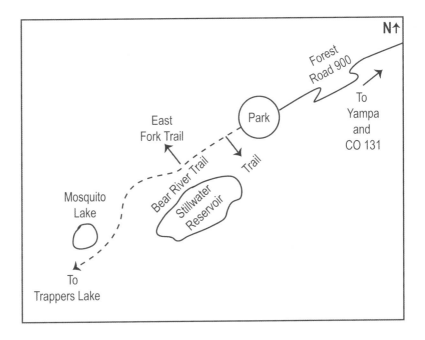

35   The Loch

Hike Distance: 2.4 miles each way

Hiking Time: Up in 62 minutes. Down in 56 minutes.

Starting Elevation: 9,270 feet

Highest Elevation: 10,180 feet

Elevation Gain: 1,000 feet (includes 45 extra feet each way)

Trail: All the way

Relevant Maps: Trails Illustrated 200 or 301

  McHenrys Peak 7½ minute

  Larimer County Number Three

  Rocky Mountain National Park

*The Loch and the
Sharkstooth beyond*

You can hardly go wrong hiking in Rocky Mountain National Park. The trails are well-marked and maintained. Pets and vehicles are excluded from the trails, and the surroundings are breathtaking. The one problem may be the crowds. Avoiding the weekends and getting an early start can lessen this problem. Late June is an ideal time for a hike to the Loch since the flowing water is so abundant. It will probably not be until mid-July before one can hike above the Loch to the Lake of Glass and Sky Pond without snow blocking the trail.

Getting There: Drive to the Glacier Gorge parking area, which is 8.8 miles from the Beaver Meadows entrance to Rocky Mountain National Park by way of Bear Lake Road. If unable to park here, additional parking is available farther up the road near Bear Lake.

The Hike: Start from the Glacier Gorge parking area and ascend southwest to the trailhead sign. Take the left fork toward Alberta Falls and a quick right fork at a sign toward Loch Vale. In 0.6 mile you will pass impressive Alberta Falls on the left. After another 0.6 mile from the falls take a right fork at a sign and a very quick left fork to stay on the main trail, which ascends to the right of the creek. The rushing water provides many scenic falls. In 1.2 miles from the last fork, you will emerge at the lovely Loch. Take some refreshment, admire the scenery, and feed the eager Jays at the lake. The Sharkstooth is the huge mountain to the south-southwest across the lake. Thatchtop Mountain looms above to your left (south-southeast). Return as you ascended and be sure to take the correct forks.

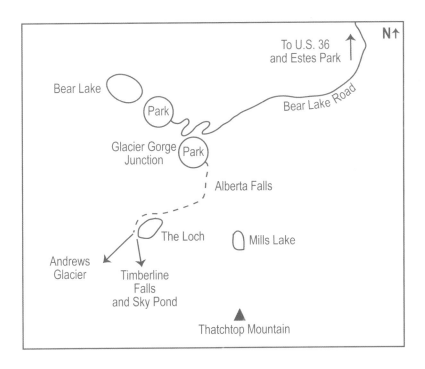

36 Ute Trail to Timberline Pass

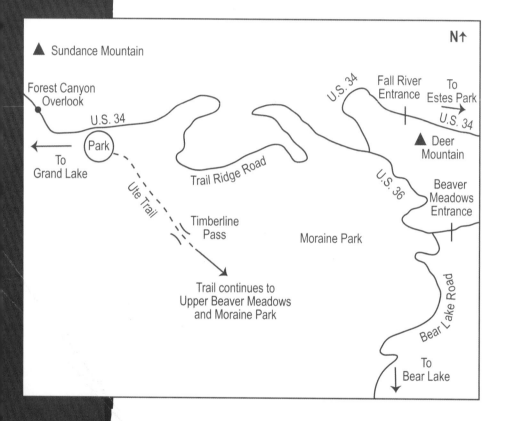

N↑

▲ Sundance Mountain

Forest Canyon
Overlook

U.S. 34

U.S. 34

Fall River
Entrance

To
Estes Park

U.S. 34

← To
Grand Lake

Park

▲ Deer
Mountain

Ute Trail

Trail Ridge Road

U.S. 36

Beaver
Meadows
Entrance

Timberline
Pass

Moraine Park

Trail continues to
Upper Beaver Meadows
and Moraine Park

Bear Lake Road

To
Bear Lake
↓

H ere is an easy hike, which is totally above timberline and begins from the extraordinary Trail Ridge Road in Rocky Mountain National Park. Avoid the crowds of visitors by going during the week or when school is in session.

Getting There: Drive to the intersection of U.S. 36 and U.S. 34 at Deer Ridge Junction. This is the eastern entrance to Trail Ridge Road. Drive up Trail Ridge Road, which is U.S. 34, for 10.3 miles and park on the left near an informational sign about the Ute Trail.

The Hike: Begin from the sign on the clear Ute Trail to the southeast. Follow it over tundra with magnificent views in every direction and along the ridge for 1.8 miles down to a rock formation on the left side of the cairn-marked trail. This is the unmarked Timberline Pass. The trail now descends toward the trees and will continue to Upper Beaver Meadows and Moraine Park. The panorama of Longs Peak and the adjacent mountains from the trail is very special. Unless you have a car waiting at Upper Beaver Meadows, retrace your route back to Trail Ridge Road. (From Trail Ridge Road, the Ute Trail extends 6.5 miles southeast down to Upper Beaver Meadows.)

Hike Distance: 1.8 miles each way

Hiking Time: Out in 48 minutes. Back in 48 minutes.

Starting Elevation: 11,365 feet

Highest Elevation: 11,660 feet

Elevation Gain: 765 feet (includes 470 extra feet)

Trail: All the way

Relevant Maps: Trails Illustrated 200 and 301

Trail Ridge 7½ minute

Larimer County Number Three

Rocky Mountain National Park (available at entrance station)

Views From the Pass: ESE to Twin Sisters Peaks

S to Hallett Peak

SSE to Mount Meeker, Longs Peak, Pagoda Mountain, Chiefs Head Peak, McHenrys Peak

SE to Estes Cone

37 Long Lake, Round Lake, and Lake Percy

Here is a gentle hike to three lakes north of Rabbit Ears Pass along the Continental Divide. An extensive network of dirt roads and trails emanates from Buffalo Pass to reach many peaks and lakes such as these three. Motorized vehicles are forbidden on this route.

Getting There: Drive to Buffalo Pass northeast of Steamboat Springs via Routt County Road 38 and Forest Road 60. From Buffalo Pass, drive south on Road 310 for 4.8 miles, just past Fish Creek Reservoir on the right to a road barrier and park nearby off the road. Regular cars can readily reach this trailhead on these wide, well-graded, unpaved roads.

The Hike: Start walking south-southeast around the barrier up the wide road. Within 200 yards go left at a T. After another 0.7 mile you reach a fork. The road descending right will lead down to Fish Creek Falls several miles farther. You take the left fork and soon will see Long Lake below on your right, before leaving the road and going left (east-southeast) on Fish Creek Trail. Ascend into the forest for 0.8 mile and reach a four-way intersection. The Continental Divide Trail passes left to Buffalo Pass on the Wyoming Trail and right to the Base Camp Trailhead. Continue straight (east-northeast) another 100 yards to lovely Round Lake and 200 yards farther to equally appealing Lake Percy. Both lakes are graced with water lilies in mid-summer. The trail continues to an eastern trailhead but Lake Percy is your far point. Take care to make the correct choices at trail intersections on your way back to the trailhead near Fish Creek Reservoir.

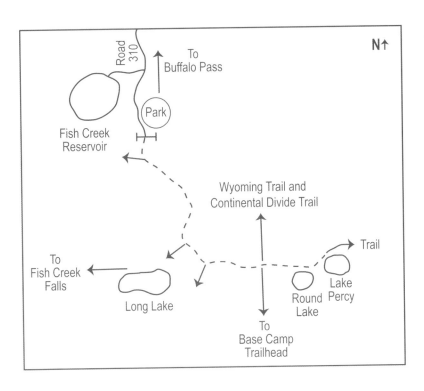

Road 310

To Buffalo Pass

N↑

Park

Fish Creek Reservoir

Wyoming Trail and Continental Divide Trail

Trail

To Fish Creek Falls

Long Lake

Round Lake

Lake Percy

To Base Camp Trailhead

Hike Distance: 2.6 miles each way

Hiking Time: Out in 55 minutes. Back in 54 minutes.

Starting Elevation: 9,920 feet

Highest Elevation: 10,110 feet

Elevation Gain: 640 feet (includes 225 extra feet each way)

Trail: All the way

Relevant Maps: Trails Illustrated 118

    Mount Werner 7½ minute

    Routt County Number Two

    Jackson County Number Three

    Routt National Forest

38 Pavilion Point

View from Pavilion Point Trail

This trail uses the old railroad bed of the Argentine Central Railroad, which continued up Leavenworth Gulch to Waldorf. Aspen and many trail junctions abound on this hike.

Getting There: From I-70 at Silver Plume take Exit 226. On the unpaved frontage road on the south side of I-70 drive west for 0.4 mile and park.

The Hike: Begin southeast up the trail at signs. Stay on the main, well-marked trail for 1.2 miles as you pass a water tank on the left and an old mine remnant on the right. Keep straight at a four-way intersection and avoid a side trail on the right. At the 1.2-mile mark you will reach a fork. A mine ruin can be seen ahead on the left, but ascend sharply right. Soon pass a side road on the left. Continue on the main trail. Go straight at a four-way junction and soon ascend sharply to the left. Ascend 0.75 mile and reach a chimney remnant, which marks Pavilion Point where train travelers used to visit. From an overlook above to the left there are some good views.

Hike Distance: 2.5 miles each way

Hiking Time: Up in 70 minutes. Down in 60 minutes.

Starting Elevation: 9,170 feet

Highest Elevation: 10,000 feet

Elevation Gain: 896 feet (includes 33 extra feet each way)

Trail: All the way

Relevant Maps: Trails Illustrated 104

Georgetown 7½ minute

Clear Creek County

Arapaho National Forest

Views From the Summit: NW to Stanley Mountain

SW to Pendleton Mountain

W to Mount Sniktau

WNW to Republican Mountain

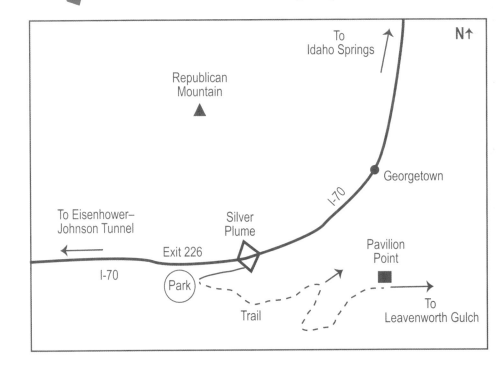

39 Charles Peak

Hike Distance: 1.5 miles each way

Hiking Time: Up in 60 minutes. Down in 30 minutes.

Starting Elevation: 11,180 feet

Highest Elevation: 12,050 feet

Elevation Gain: 946 feet (includes 38 extra feet each way)

Trail: All the way until the final 100 yards

Relevant Maps: Trails Illustrated 126

Crooked Creek Pass 7½ minute

Eagle County Number Three

White River National Forest

Views From the Summit: NE to Gold Dust Peak

ESE to Fools Peak

SSW to Pyramid Peak and the Maroon Bells

WSW to Mount Sopris

View of Fools Peak from Charles Peak

This hike is the easier of two trails to Charles Peak in the Holy Cross Wilderness. Starting at the Peter Estin Hut, the trail rises steeply to tree line and the nearby open summit. From the top on a clear day the views are outstanding.

Getting There: From I-70 take Exit 147 and drive south 0.4 mile into the town of Eagle. Turn left from U.S. 6 on Capitol Street and follow it south to an intersection with Brush Creek Road. Go left and stay on this road (Eagle County 307) past Sylvan Lake to Crooked Creek Pass, which is 20.7 miles south of Exit 147 from I-70. Ascend the left fork and avoid roads on the right at miles 2.9 and 3.1 from the pass. At mile 5.0 park on the right near the Peter Estin Hut.

The Hike: Start out to the northeast past a road barrier and quickly pass the Peter Estin Hut on the left. This hut is one of the Tenth Mountain Division's network of high mountain huts, which can be rented all year round. Avoid the hut and respect the privacy of those who have rented it. Follow the trail to the east and pass a register. Keep right (east) at a fork. A sign states that you are on the Iron Edge Trail. Continue steeply upward and pass a Holy Cross Wilderness sign as the terrain opens as you approach tree line. The Charles Peak summit will be seen above the trail on the left. At the high point of the trail, leave it and ascend north over tundra to a benchmark and glorious views at the top of Charles Peak. Your return will be much faster than the ascent.

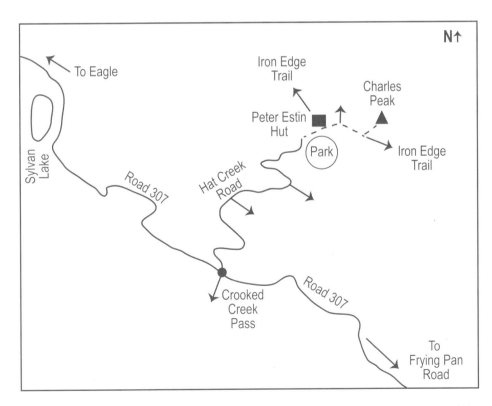

40 Crag Crest Trail— East Trailhead to Ridge Top

Hike Distance: 2.0 miles each way

Hiking Time: Up in 54 minutes. Down in 40 minutes.

Starting Elevation: 10,125 feet

Highest Elevation: 11,129 feet

Elevation Gain: 1,040 feet (includes 18 extra feet each way)

Trail: All the way

Relevant Maps: Trails Illustrated 136

    Grand Mesa 7½ minute

    Delta County Number Two

    Grand Mesa National Forest

Views From the Summit: S to Butts Lake and Lone Cone

    SSE to Mount Sneffels

    SSW to Eggleston Lake

    SE to Bullfinch Reservoirs One and Two, Uncompahgre Peak, Wetterhorn Peak

G rand Mesa is a wonderful year-round playground. There are dozens of lakes and many hiking and cross-country ski trails. One of these paths is the Crag Crest Trail, which has been designated a National Recreational Trail and provides an 11-mile loop through and above many adjacent lakes. Here is a short hike that provides a good taste of this beautiful trail.

Getting There: Drive south on CO 65 from Exit 49 off I-70 east of Grand Junction. Follow this paved road through Mesa and keep right at mile 10.2. Keep on CO 65 and pass the western trailhead of the Crag Crest Trail at mile 33.4. Drive 1 mile farther to Carp Lake on your left and turn left off of CO 65 on a paved road, which will lead to Eggleston Lake. Park at mile 3.4 from CO 65 on the right at a designated area alongside Eggleston Lake.

The Hike: Walk northeast on the road for 125 yards from the parking area and then ascend the trail on the left (north). Cross an open area into the trees and after a few hundred yards keep straight at a four-way trail intersection. In 0.3 mile farther, take a left fork at Upper Eggleston Lake and in another 0.5 mile pass Bullfinch Reservoir Number One on your right. Within 200 more yards keep right at a fork and sign. Butts Lake is near on the left. Ascend some switchbacks and go through a field of volcanic rock to reach a high point of the ridge and a panorama of the Grand Mesa. This is the terminus of this trail description but you may wish to continue farther or even complete the entire loop. Enjoy!

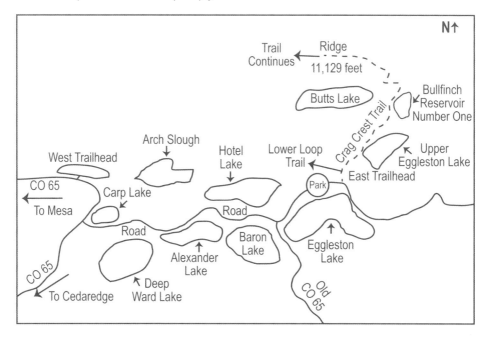

41 Upper Fish Creek Falls

A popular National Recreational Trail leads past Lower Fish Creek Falls to the Upper Falls on the outskirts of Steamboat Springs. The excellent trail is steep but these two waterfalls are worth the effort. A fee is required at the trailhead parking area. Bikes are permitted on the trail and dogs must be kept on a leash.

Getting There: In central Steamboat Springs at Lincoln Avenue (U.S. 40), drive north on Third Street and turn right at the first intersection onto Fish Creek Road. Follow this paved road for 3.1 miles from U.S. 40 to an entry fee station and parking lot at road end.

The Hike: Start down and northeast from the parking area. Reach a bridge and spectacular views of the photogenic Lower Fish Creek Falls. Continue up the steep trail through an aspen forest. Eventually the trail passes along a ledge with Fish Creek below on your left. At mile 1.6 cross the creek on a wooden bridge and continue to ascend several switchbacks. This time the trail passes along a rocky ledge with the creek down on your right. At mile 2.2 Upper Fish Creek Falls comes into view on the left as the trail sharply curves left and continues almost 3 more miles up the valley to Long Lake. Enjoy the falls and the cascading water above and below before your quicker return.

Hike Distance: 2.2 miles each way

Hiking Time: Up in 69 minutes. Down in 48 minutes.

Starting Elevation: 7,480 feet

Highest Elevation: 8,880 feet

Elevation Gain: 1,610 feet (includes 105 extra feet each way)

Trail: All the way

Relevant Maps: Trails Illustrated 118

    Steamboat Springs 7½ minute

    Mount Werner 7½ minute

    Routt County Number Four

    Routt National Forest

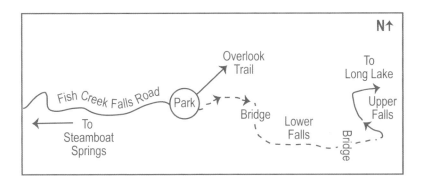

42 Hahns Peak

Just 15 miles south of the Wyoming border, Hahns Peak, with its impressive summit, is a satisfying but remote hiking destination. There are two major routes to the summit. One (here described) uses a hiking trail and is more direct. The other traverses an old mining road to the base of the summit ridge and the former Tom Thumb Mine and is a mile longer. A lookout tower lies at the summit and has some great vistas.

Getting There: From the western edge of Steamboat Springs, drive northwest on Routt County Road 129 and pass through Clark and the town of Hahns Peak and arrive at the hamlet of Columbine at mile 28.9 from U.S. 40. At Columbine leave the paved road and turn right onto Road 490. Drive straight up this rough road for 1 mile and turn left at a fork. Park within 50 yards in a clearing by some trees and a trailhead sign. Hahns Peak can be seen looming above a cabin ruin from there. Regular cars with reasonable clearance can reach this parking area.

The Hike: From the trailhead parking area, follow the rough road and avoid a left fork as it ascends through intermittent forest for 0.5 mile to the north to a junction with a sign. Take the trail on the right and leave the road. Continue south up to a ridge and eventually meet the mining road that you left at the trail sign. (Four-wheel drivers can reach this point on the road.) This is timberline for this peak. Continue on any of several trails that lead up the talus past mine ruins to the ridge that ends at the summit lookout tower. On your descent be careful to take the correct forks and use your compass. It is easy to become lost on this mountain.

Hike Distance: 2.0 miles each way

Hiking Time: Up in 80 minutes.
Down in 45 minutes.

Starting Elevation: 9,400 feet

Highest Elevation: 10,839 feet

Elevation Gain: 1,549 feet
(includes 55 extra feet each way)

Trail: All the way

Relevant Maps: Trails Illustrated 116

Hahns Peak 7½ minute

Routt County Number Two

Routt National Forest

Views From the Summit: S to Hahns
Peak Village and Steamboat Lake

SE to Pearl Lake

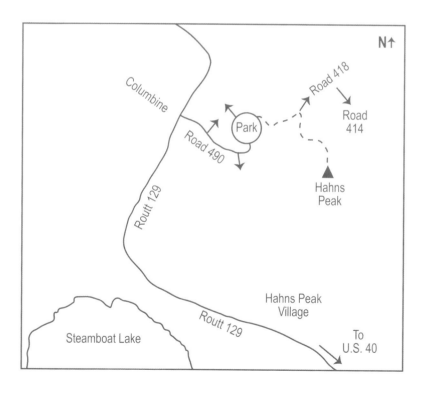

43   Spruce Mountain

View south from Spruce Mountain

Beautiful forest, a well-marked trail, rock formations, and wide vistas from the summit are features of this Douglas County hike. There is no fee, dogs must be on a leash, and motorized vehicles are forbidden.

Getting There: From I-25 south of Denver take Exit 173 and follow Spruce Mountain Road through Larkspur 5.7 miles and park in the Spruce Mountain lot on the right. Access is also possible from I-25 via Exit 167 and Noe Road.

The Hike: Begin west from the parking area on the clear trail and go left at a signed fork after several hundred yards. The trail winds around the mountain and reaches the beginning of a loop after 1.6 miles. For a clockwise route, continue left to reach Windy Point at the summit of Spruce Mountain at the 2.7-mile mark. Palmer Park and Mount Herman can be seen to the south and flat plains to the southeast. Continue as the trail leads to the left to descend to another signed fork. Ascend to the right and complete the loop and return by your ascent route.

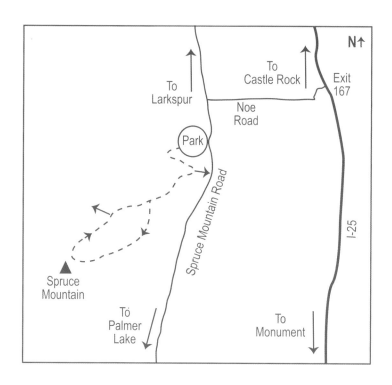

Hike Distance: 5.5 miles (total loop)

Hiking Time: Up in 62 minutes. Down in 62 minutes.

Starting Elevation: 7,120 feet

Highest Elevation: 7,605 feet

Elevation Gain: 629 feet (includes 144 extra feet)

Trail: All the way

Relevant Maps: Spruce Mountain (Internet)

Larkspur 7½ minute

Douglas County Number Two

Views From the Summit: S to Palmer Park and Mount Herman

44 Diamond Peak

Mount Richthofen and Nokhu Crags from Diamond Peak

Cameron Pass is named after General R. A. Cameron, who founded the city of Fort Collins. These peaks are 30 miles south of Wyoming and are part of the Medicine Bow or Rawah Mountain Range. This hike leads to the highest of several peaks along a ridge.

Getting There: Drive on CO 14 between Fort Collins on the east and Walden on the west to Cameron Pass. Park in the lot on the west side of the pass near a picnic ground.

The Hike: Start out west-southwest into the trees and find the trail. Ascend with a creek on the right. As you enter an open basin below the Diamond Peaks the trail fades away. Proceed to the ridge on the south side of the highest peak to the northwest. This peak has a distinctive hump near the top. A benchmark and cairn mark the summit. Enjoy the vistas before descending directly down southeast to the trail you left in the basin.

Hike Distance: 1.4 miles on the ascent. 1.1 miles on the descent.

Hiking Time: Up in 66 minutes. Down in 33 minutes.

Starting Elevation: 10,276 feet

Highest Elevation: 11,852 feet

Elevation Gain: 1,576 feet

Trail: First half only

Relevant Maps: Trails Illustrated 112

    Clark Peak 7½ minute

    Larimer County Number Three

    Roosevelt National Forest

Views From the Summit: NNE to Cameron Peak

    ESE to Iron Mountain

    S to Mount Richthofen

    SE to Longs Peak and the Nokhu Crags

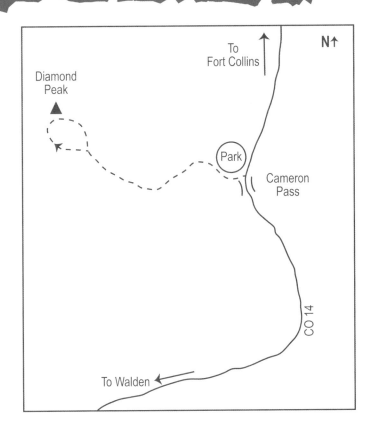

45 Royal Mountain

Royal Mountain lies south of the town of Frisco. The trail to the top is short but steep and traverses the site of Masontown, which was settled in the 1860s by a group from a town of the same name in Pennsylvania. Masontown was destroyed by an avalanche in 1926.

Getting There: Drive to Main Street in Frisco. The large trailhead parking area lies 30 yards east of I-70 (Exit 201) or 0.8 mile west of CO 9 on the south side of Main Street.

The Hike: From the parking area, begin southeast and cross Tenmile Creek on a bridge. No more flowing water will be encountered. Continue left on the paved bike path that connects Breckenridge with Frisco, Copper Mountain, and Vail. After 0.3 mile from your starting point, you reach signs on the right. One says Mount Royal and the other tells the history of Masontown. Your route to Royal Mountain will pass through its remnants.

Leave the bike path and enter the trees to the right (south). Follow the main clear trail as it rises, steeply at times, to the south. Avoid any side trails and continue to ascend. After 0.5 mile from the bike path, there is a small clearing and remnants of Masontown. Avoid the trail on the left and continue straight (south-southwest) almost another mile up to an unmarked fork. Go to the right (northwest) another 0.2 mile to a ridge overlook of Tenmile Canyon. A trail continues along the ridge to the right (north) a final 0.2 mile to the unmarked high point. Trees obstruct views to the south and east. Buffalo Mountain can be seen to the north-northeast and Uneva Peak to the west-southwest. Return as you ascended. There are no good shortcuts on the descent.

Hike Distance: 2.1 miles each way

Hiking Time: Up in 60 minutes. Down in 40 minutes.

Starting Elevation: 9,095 feet

Highest Elevation: 10,502 feet

Elevation Gain: 1,477 feet (includes 35 extra feet each way)

Trail: All the way

Relevant Maps:

Trails Illustrated 108

Frisco 7½ minute

Summit County Number Two

Arapaho National Forest—Dillon Ranger District

Views From the Summit:

NNE to Ptarmigan Peak

NNW to Buffalo Mountain

NE to Lake Dillon

S to Peak 1

SE to Bald Mountain

WSW to Uneva Peak

View south from Royal Mountain

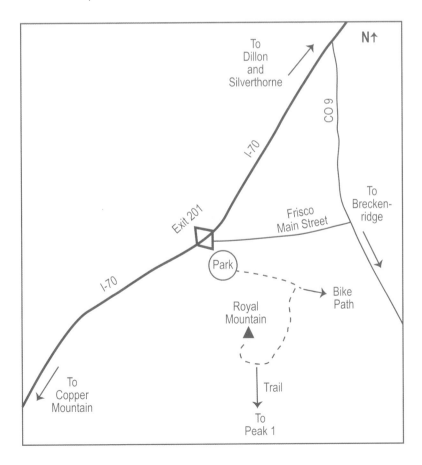

99

46 Silver Lake

Hike Distance: 1.6 miles each way

Hiking Time: Up in 69 minutes. Down in 56 minutes.

Starting Elevation: 10,320 feet

Highest Elevation: 11,788 feet

Elevation Gain: 1,528 feet (includes 30 extra feet each way)

Trail: All the way

Relevant Maps: Trails Illustrated 141

Telluride 7½ minute

San Miguel County Number Three

Uncompahgre National Forest

Sara Markey relaxes at Silver Lake

The hiking trail to Silver Lake, east of Telluride, is short but one of the steepest you are likely to encounter. However, beautiful, clear Silver Lake and Silver Basin make your effort worthwhile.

The trail can be accessed by four-wheel drive, and the hike will be described from this high point above Bridal Veil Falls where Black Bear Road becomes one way. Without four-wheel drive, one can park 1.9 miles from East Colorado Avenue and South Willow Street at the beginning of Black Bear Road and walk up the road for 2.4 miles to the trailhead.

Getting There: Drive east from East Colorado Avenue and South Willow Street in Telluride for 1.9 miles and reach the beginning of Black Bear Road. With four-wheel drive, ascend Black Bear Road for 2.4 more miles to a fork and park. Black Bear Road becomes one-way coming toward you on the left.

The Hike: Begin to the west-southwest past a vehicular barrier and follow a road past a nice home and a power facility on the right. At 0.5 mile from the trailhead, leave the road and cross Bridal Veil Creek with a large boulder on the right. Ascend the primitive, very steep trail that will eventually angle up to the west-northwest into the forest. Several side trails will be encountered. Always take the ascending main trail. After almost a mile of laborious ascent, enter a meadow and soon you will see a waterfall emerging from Silver Lake above. Another 200 feet of elevation brings you to lovely Silver Lake with Ballard Mountain to the south-southwest and La Junta Peak to the south. As you retrace your descent route, be very careful as loose gravel can undermine footing. Hiking poles can be helpful. The views across Bridal Veil Basin and toward Black Bear Pass and Telluride Peak are special.

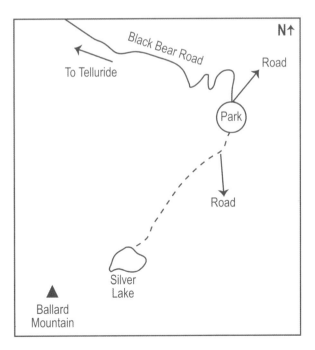

47 Lake Katherine

Hike Distance: 2.4 miles each way

Hiking Time: Up in 68 minutes.
Down in 50 minutes.

Starting Elevation: 8,915 feet

Highest Elevation: 9,884 feet

Elevation Gain: 1,544 feet
(includes 575 extra feet)

Trail: All the way

Relevant Maps: Trails Illustrated
116 & 117

Mount Ethel 7½ minute

Mount Zirkel 7½ minute

Pitchpine Mountain 7½ minute

Jackson County Number One

Routt National Forest

S ome lakes are more striking than others. Lake Katherine ranks high in natural beauty. The teal-colored water, the green, partially timbered bowl above it, and the remnants of an old dam at its outlet make this body of water special. Within the Mount Zirkel Wilderness and below the Continental Divide, this short hike is quite popular.

Getting There: From CO 14 at the southern edge of Walden, drive west on Jackson County Road 12W. Keep left at mile 7.7, go right at mile 9.8, and at mile 11.9 turn left at a T onto Jackson Road 16. Follow this good, dirt road until it ends at the trailhead at mile 19.6 from CO 14 and park.

The Hike: Walk west on the Lone Pine Trail (Number 1129) into the forest. Quickly pass through a stile and soon pass through a meadow before entering the wilderness area. After another smaller meadow, you reach two signed forks. Keep left at each. The first right fork continues to the Continental Divide and the second leads to Bighorn Lake and beyond.

After continuing south on the second left fork, make a significant, unassisted, creek crossing before ascending more steeply. The cascading waters from Lake Katherine will impress you soon on your left as the clear trail rises to the lake. When lovely Lake Katherine comes into view, take a left fork toward its outflow. A trail on the right leads to some campsites. You may want to linger awhile at this beautiful lake.

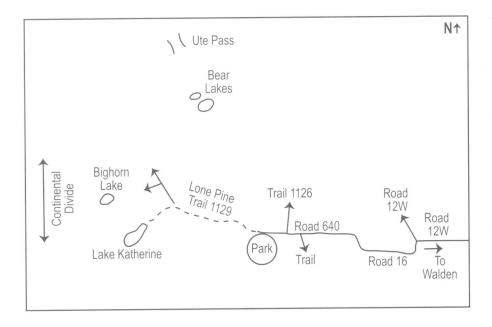

Mount Flora— Colorado Mines Peak Saddle

"Keyhole Lake" below the saddle

Hike Distance: 1.7 miles each way

Hiking Time: Up in 48 minutes. Down in 35 minutes.

Starting Elevation: 11,315 feet

Highest Elevation: 12,140 feet

Elevation Gain: 925 feet (includes 50 extra feet each way)

Trail: All the way

Relevant Maps: Trails Illustrated 103

Berthoud Pass 7½ minute

Grand County Number Four

Arapaho National Forest

This hike brings you quickly to sweeping vistas along the Continental Divide Trail. If you are inclined, you may wish to continue up to Mount Flora as the Continental Divide Trail continues on to Bill Moore Lake and James Peak.

Getting There: Drive on U.S. 40 to Berthoud Pass (NW of Empire and SE of Winter Park) and park in the lot on the east side.

The Hike: Start out up the wide road to the southeast as it rises by switchbacks 0.8 mile to the Continental Divide Trail sign on the left as the road curves right. Mount Flora is 2 miles farther. Follow the good Continental Divide Trail another 0.9 mile up to a saddle between Colorado Mines Peak on the right and a subpeak of Mount Flora on the left. The keyhole-shaped lake below to the east-southeast is unnamed. Enjoy the great scenery.

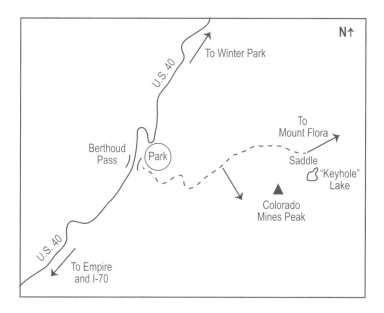

49 Boulder Canyon Overlook

Hike Distance: 2.7 miles each way

Hiking Time: Up in 62 minutes. Down in 52 minutes.

Starting Elevation: 7,300 feet

Highest Elevation: 8,060 feet

Elevation Gain: 1,000 feet
(includes 120 extra feet each way)

Trail: All the way

Relevant Maps: Trails Illustrated 100

Walker Ranch (available at trailhead)

Eldorado Springs 7½ minute

Boulder County

Boulder County Open Space

Roosevelt National Forest

Views From the Overlook: NNW to Estes Cone, Mummy Mountain, Twin Sisters Peak

NW to Bald Mountain, Chiefs Head Mountain, Pagoda Mountain, Longs Peak, Mount Meeker

W to South Arapahoe Peak

WNW to Mount Audubon

SE to Eldorado Mountain

*North from
Boulder Canyon
Overlook*

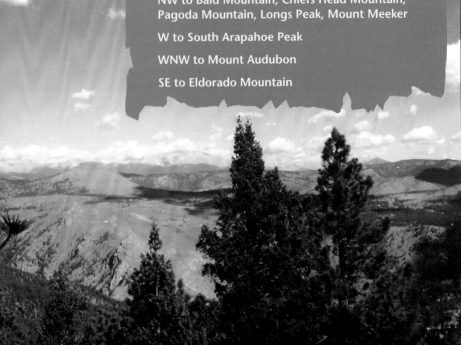

A ccess to Walker Ranch, which is part of the Boulder Open Space, is free. However, dogs must be kept on a leash, and hunting and motorized vehicles are forbidden. The ranch offers 12 miles of trails. This one gradually goes up Meyers Gulch
to a scenic overlook of Boulder Canyon and the peaks beyond. The season for this
hike is usually April through November. James Walker came from Missouri in 1869
and accumulated many parcels of land over the next 25 years. He bought the Meyers
Homestead along Meyers Gulch.

Getting There: From the intersection of Broadway and Baseline Road in south
Boulder, drive west on Baseline Road, which becomes Flagstaff Road, for 8.1 miles
and park in the Meyers Gulch parking area on the right at the trailhead at the lower
parking area.

The Hike: Begin down to the west through open terrain and then rise through
a series of grassy meadows as the trail curves clockwise to the overlook. At 0.5 mile
from the trailhead, a scenic skeleton of an old barn is passed on the left. Continuing
upward on the main Meyers Homestead Trail, a trail enters from the right before you
ascend more steeply through groves of aspen both to the left and right of the trail. A
steep trail segment then rises to more level terrain and a sign marking the terminus of
this hike at the overlook. This is a good place for some peak recognition before your
return. Longs Peak can be seen to the northwest. South Arapaho Peak lies to the west
and Mount Audubon to the west-northwest.

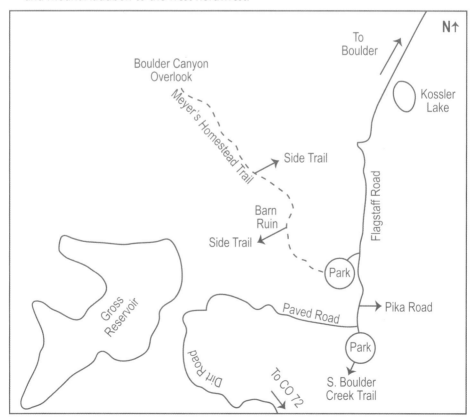

50 Kenosha Pass to Guernsey Creek

This is a great hike for aspen trees and panoramic views of South Park. The route from Kenosha Pass to Guernsey Creek uses a segment of the well-marked Colorado Trail that extends a total distance of 469 miles from Denver to Durango.

Getting There: Drive on U.S. 285 to Kenosha Pass and park on the west side of the road near the entrance to Kenosha Pass Campground. Kenosha Pass is 19 miles southwest of Bailey and 4 miles northeast of Jefferson.

The Hike: Start west-southwest from the parking area and take two left forks in the first few hundred yards. Then reach the actual trailhead with Colorado Trail signs and proceed west on the trail. Ascend gently through many aspen trees and reach a high point after 0.75 mile from the trailhead. Then descend through a series of open areas with great views of South Park and the mountains to the west. Eventually cross a dirt road and continue west and down to small Guernsey Creek at 9,870 feet. This is a good spot for some refreshment and the terminus of the hike. The Colorado Trail continues west to the Michigan Creek Road and up to Georgia Pass as it meanders through Colorado.

Hike Distance: 2.5 miles each way

Hiking Time: Out in 64 minutes. Back in 57 minutes.

Starting Elevation: 10,000 feet

Highest Elevation: 10,360 feet

Lowest Elevation: 9,870 feet (includes 600 extra feet due to trail undulations)

Elevation Gain: 960 feet (includes 110 extra feet)

Trail: All the way

Relevant Maps: Trails Illustrated 105

Jefferson 7½ minute

Colorado Trail Map Number Five

Park County Number One

Pike National Forest

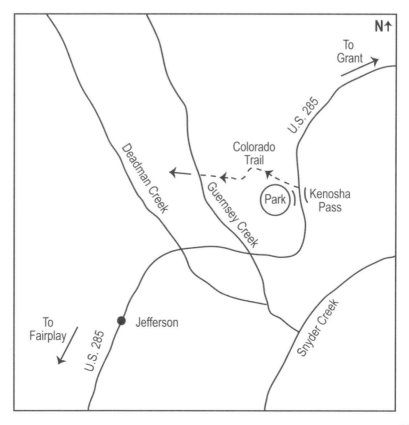

51 Chinns Lake, Sherwin Lake, and Slater Lake

Slater Lake, Fall River Reservoir, Chinns Lake, and Sherwin Lake (clockwise from left)

Hike Distance: 2.0 miles each way

Hiking Time: Up in 68 minutes. Down in 55 minutes.

Starting Elevation: 10,400 feet

Highest Elevation: 11,395 feet

Elevation Gain: 1,045 feet (includes 50 extra feet)

Trail: All the way until the final 100 yards

Relevant Maps: Trails Illustrated 103

   Empire 7½ minute

   Clear Creek County

   Arapaho National Forest

This easy hike to three lakes is less than 50 miles from central Denver. Gentle grassy slopes of the Continental Divide surround this outing and invite the hiker to proceed above Slater Lake, the highest of the three lakes.

Getting There: From west of Idaho Springs on I-70, take Exit 238 and drive north on Fall River Road for 6.8 miles. Then take the unpaved road on the left as Fall River Road turns sharply to the right. Follow this rough, main, dirt road up the valley for 2.4 miles and park off-road at a fork. Two metal poles flank the road straight ahead. Most regular cars can reach this point.

The Hike: Start walking up the left fork of the road to the west-southwest. Follow the main road as it rises steeply to a fork just before Chinns Lake. Go left around an abandoned cabin at Chinns Lake and continue a few hundred yards to the dam at Sherwin Lake. Witter Peak is the imposing mountain to the southwest. Continue north across the dam and follow the road as it rises steeply to the right and then switches back up into the trees. Within 100 feet after entering the forest, the main trail begins to descend. Go left here (west-northwest) on a footpath. Follow this faint trail generally up to the northwest to reach lovely, isolated Slater Lake. If you lose the trail below the lake, head toward Mount Eva to the west-northwest, find the creek emanating from Slater Lake and follow it to the lake. On your return, remember how you ascended from the dam at Sherwin Lake.

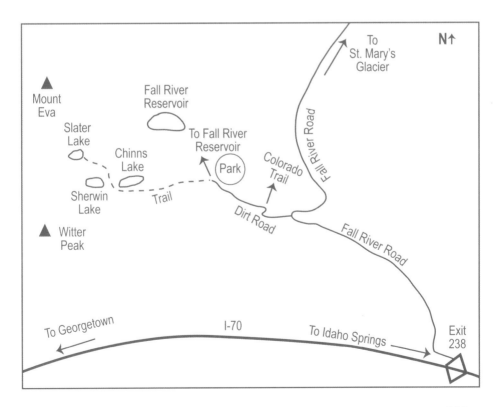

52 Mount McConnel

Located in the lovely lower Poudre Valley, Mount McConnel can be climbed most of the year due to its modest elevation. There are two loop trails on the mountain. The lower loop is the Kreutzer Nature Trail, named after an early U.S. Forest Ranger in this area. The upper loop is the Summit Trail and is longer. In the spring, watch out for ticks. The Mount McConnel Trail is designated a National Recreational Trail.

Getting There: From U.S. 287 northwest of Fort Collins, drive west on CO 14 through the very scenic Poudre Canyon for 23 miles and either park on the left if the bridge is blocked (north side of river but south of CO 14) or drive 250 yards to the trailhead signboard and park nearby.

The Hike: The trail begins to the east and soon curves right, crosses a road and reaches a signed fork after 0.9 mile. This is the upper edge of the Kreutzer Trail. Take the Summit Trail on the right and ascent another 1.3 miles to a fork near the summit. Take the trail up to the right the final 0.2 mile to a large, unmarked, summit boulder with a few embedded trees. There are good vistas to the south and west. Return by your ascent route unless you wish to continue the longer Summit Trail loop back to connect with the Kreutzer Loop.

Hike Distance: 2 miles each way.

Hiking Time: Up in 63 minutes. Down in 56 minutes.

Starting Elevation: 6,646 feet

Highest Elevation: 7,980 feet

Elevation Gain: 1,524 feet (includes 190 extra feet)

Trail: All the way

Relevant Maps: Trails Illustrated 101

    Big Narrows 7½ minute

    Larimer County Number Two

    Roosevelt National Forest

Views From the Summit: S to West White Pine Mountain

    SW to Comanche Peak

    WNW to South, Middle and North Bald Mountains

    WSW to South and North Rawah Peaks

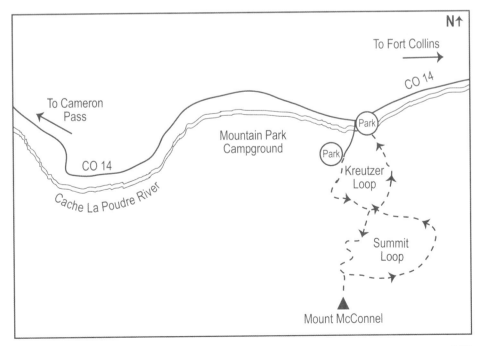

53 The Crags (Pikes Peak Region)

This hike to the Crags is ideal for all ages and takes you through some of the most impressive rock formations in Colorado. The trail ends at an overlook point with magnificent views to the north and the Pikes Peak Massif to the southeast. There are many rocky towers to explore around trail's end but be careful. The usual season for hiking this trail is from May into late October. The route also makes a reasonable cross-country ski tour or snowshoe trek in the winter.

Getting There: From the junction of U.S. 24 and CO 67 in Divide (west of Colorado Springs), drive south on CO 67 for 4.3 miles and turn left onto unpaved Teller County Road 62. Follow this occasionally bumpy road for 3.1 miles and turn left into the Crags Campground. Drive 0.3 mile through the campground to trailhead parking at the end of the road. En route to this point take a right fork on Teller 62 at mile 1.6. Regular cars can reach the trailhead parking area.

The Hike: Begin to the east past a trail register and continue up through a scenic valley with many beautiful rocks above the trail. After passing through an open area, the path enters the trees and curves north and northeast to reach a group of boulders at the end of the trail. Savor the views and perhaps some careful rock exploration before returning as you ascended.

Hike Distance: 2.3 miles each way

Hiking Time: Up in 55 minutes. Down in 46 minutes.

Starting Elevation: 10,100 feet

Highest Elevation: 10,760 feet

Elevation Gain: 900 feet (includes 120 extra feet each way)

Trail: All the way

Relevant Maps: Trails Illustrated 137

Pikes Peak 7½ minute

Woodland Park 7½ minute

El Paso County Number One

Pike National Forest

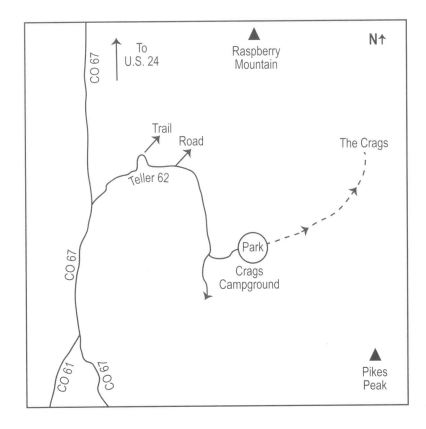

54 Ouzel Falls

The Wild Basin Hike to Ouzel Falls in Rocky Mountain National Park is one of the best flowing-water outings in Colorado. An entry fee is required and no pets or vehicles are allowed on the excellent well-marked trails. The best time for this trek is when the spring run-off is still full.

Getting There: From the west side of Lyons, at the intersection of U.S. 36 and CO 7, drive west and north on CO 7 for 21.2 miles and turn left at the sign to the Wild Basin Ranger Station. After 0.4 mile on this paved road turn right onto the good dirt road, pay the entry fee, and park after 2.2 more miles at the end of the road at the Wild Basin Ranger Station. Regular cars can readily reach this point.

The Hike: Begin south-southwest from the trailhead sign and cross Hunters Creek on a bridge. After 0.3 mile on the excellent trail, pass a side trail to Copeland Falls on your left. This short side trail will add about ten minutes to your outing. Take the right fork with the raging North Saint Vrain Creek on your left. One mile past Copeland Falls, cross a large wooden bridge and admire the torrent of water as it flows by. Then ascend 0.4 mile to a series of 3 bridges at Calypso Cascades. A left fork just before these bridges leads to Finch Lake. The view up to the south from the first bridge is breathtaking. Continue over the bridges, pass through a large burn area from a 1978 fire and in 0.9 mile from the cascades, arrive at a bridge with spectacular Ouzel Falls on your left. A rough trail leads up to the left of the water to the base of the falls; an excellent place for some rest and food. The main trail continues up to Bluebird and Thunder Lakes. Return as you ascended.

Hike Distance: 2.7 miles each way

Hiking Time: Up in 65 minutes. Down in 60 minutes.

Starting Elevation: 8,500 feet

Highest Elevation: 9,400 feet

Elevation Gain: 1,150 feet (includes 125 extra feet each way)

Trail: All the way

Relevant Maps: Trails Illustrated 200 or 301

   Allens Park 7½ minute

   Boulder County

   Rocky Mountain National Park

   Roosevelt National Forest

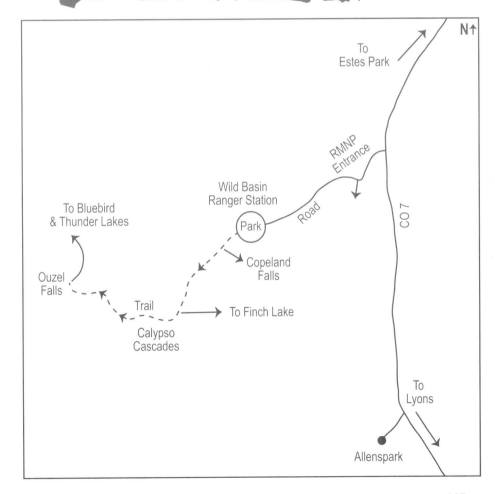

55 Eagle's View

Looking southwest from Eagle's View

Hike Distance: Up in 2.6 miles. Down in 2.8 miles.

Hiking Time: Up in 64 minutes. Down in 64 minutes.

Starting Elevation: 7,100 feet

Highest Elevation: 8,130 feet

Elevation Gain: 1,195 feet (includes 165 extra feet)

Trail: All the way

Relevant Maps: Trails Illustrated 135

    Platte Canyon 7½ minute

    Pine 7½ minute

    Jefferson County Number Two

    Reynolds Park (available at trailhead)

Views From the Summit: S to Cathedral Spires

    SSE to Raleigh Peak and Pikes Peak

    SSW to Green Mountain

Reynolds Park is one of the less-visited Jefferson County parks. However, there are good trails, picnic benches, and other amenities to serve the hiker, and particularly families. Bicycles and horses are allowed on the trails and dogs must be kept on a leash. The hike to Eagle's View, with excellent vistas to the south and west especially, can be done in a loop. A clockwise route will be described.

Getting There: On U.S. 285 in Conifer, drive southwest 0.5 mile from the intersection with CO 73 and turn south on the Foxton Road (Jefferson County Number 97). Follow this good road for 5.2 miles and park at the southernmost parking area on the right at the Songbird Trailhead.

The Hike: Begin on foot to the west on the Songbird Trail, which gradually rises 0.5 mile to an intersection. Continue to the left (southwest) on the Elkhorn Trail, which rises 100 yards to another fork. Continue straight (west-southwest). You are now on the Oxen Draw Trail, which rises steeply 0.9 mile to reach the Eagle's View Trail on the left. Ascend to the southeast another mile to the Eagle's View Overlook. This is the highest point in the park. The trail continues north to connect with the Raven's Roost Trail. Enjoy the great view of Pikes Peak (south-southeast) and some refreshment before returning back on the Eagle's View Trail to the first trail junction. To continue the loop, ascend the Raven's Roost Trail on the left (northwest). This trail curls back to rejoin the Elkhorn and Songbird Trails back to your starting point.

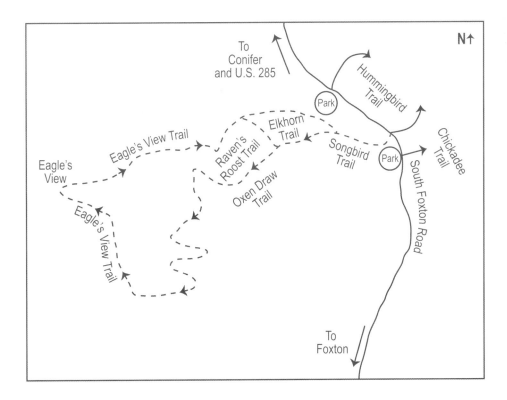

56 Flatirons Vista— Spring Brook Loop

South Boulder Peak and Bear Peak from Spring Brook Loop trail

The trails west of the Flatirons Vista loop provide great views of the peaks to the west and the plains and Boulder to the north. The clear trail is well marked and there are many side trails to explore.

Getting There: The trailhead parking area lies off the west side of CO 93, 0.3 mile south of the intersection with CO 128 between Boulder and Golden. A parking fee is required.

The Hike: Begin west on the Flatirons Vista north trail, which reaches two trails on the left and a gate after 0.9 mile. Pass through the gate and descend to a creek crossing and then rise to a signed fork and the Doudy Draw Trail on the right. Go left 0.3 mile and begin the Spring Brook Loop. A counterclockwise ascent to the right takes you through open terrain and great vistas before entering the forest and reaching a trail junction with a road above on the right. This is a good place for a break. Continue on the Spring Brook south trail and loop back to reach your ascent trail. The return to the trailhead will require some uphill trekking.

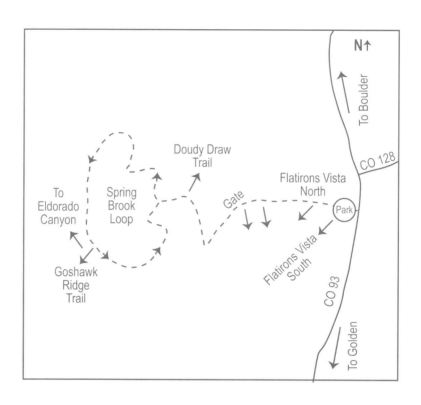

Flatirons Vista—Spring Brook Loop

Hike Distance: Out in 3.6 miles. Back in 3.5 miles.

Hiking Time: Out in 74 minutes. Back in 75 minutes.

Starting Elevation: 5,920 feet

Highest Elevation: 6,215 feet

Elevation Gain: 545 feet (includes 250 extra feet)

Trail: All the way

Relevant Maps: Doudy Draw/Eldorado Mountain
(available at trailhead)

Trails Illustrated 100

Louisville 7½ minute

Boulder County

King Lake, Betty Lake, and Bob Lake

Betty Lake seen from Bob Lake

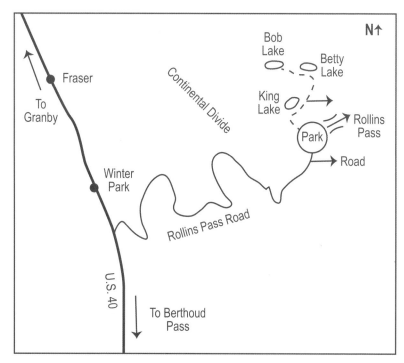

The hike from Rollins Pass to King, Betty, and Bob Lakes is gentle enough for all ages. The vistas are great and, in mid-July especially, the flowers can be extraordinary. The area is also full of history since a railroad ran over Rollins Pass until 1928 and the town of Corona was located here. This route begins high on the Continental Divide, drops to a creek crossing, and then rises to adjacent Betty and Bob Lakes.

Getting There: On U.S. 40 drive north 11.8 miles from Berthoud Pass or south from Vasquez Road in Winter Park for 1.7 miles. Then ascend Rollins Pass Road (also called Moffat Road) for 13.8 miles and park in a designated area by the sign at Rollins Pass. Stay on the main dirt road to reach this point. At a five-way intersection at mile 3.7 from U.S. 40 take the second road on the right. At a four-way intersection at mile 6.4 keep straight, and keep left at mile 13.7. Although the road gets a bit rough toward the end, regular cars can reach Rollins Pass.

The Hikes: Start on foot to the northwest from Rollins Pass and quickly gain the trail, which passes wilderness signs and the foundation of a building from the former town of Corona on the right. After 0.3 mile from Rollins Pass you will reach a pole at a trail fork. King Lake will now be visible below on the right (north). Take the right fork and descend northeast past King Lake. Follow the main trail and avoid less-defined side paths. Descend to a creek crossing followed by a sign at the fork. This creek is the lowest point of this outing. Go left and ascend a fainter trail northeast. Occasional cairns help you follow the trail through the bushes to reach serene Betty Lake. The trail continues along the left side of the lake, crosses its outlet, and becomes faint as it ascends to the left of the drainage to a bench. Then turn right, lose a little elevation and cross some boulders before reaching the edge of Bob Lake (11,580 feet) nestled in an impressive rocky cirque. Enjoy the lovely setting before retracing the route back to Rollins Pass.

Hike Distance: 2.1 miles each way

Hiking Time: Out in 64 minutes. Back in 64 minutes.

Starting Elevation: 11,660 feet

Highest Elevation: 11,690 feet

Elevation Gain: 980 feet (includes 950 extra feet)

Trail: All the way but faint over the last quarter mile

Relevant Maps: Trails Illustrated 103

   East Portal 7½ minute

   Boulder County

   Roosevelt National Forest

58 Cub Lake and The Pool Loop

Cub Lake

Hike Distance: 5.8 miles (total loop)

Hiking Time: To Cub Lake in 56 minutes. On to The Pool in 32 minutes. The Pool to Cub Lake Trailhead in 48 minutes.

Starting Elevation: 8,080 feet

Highest Elevation: 8,755 feet

Elevation Gain: 895 feet (includes 220 extra feet)

Trail: All the way

Relevant Maps: Trails Illustrated 200 or 301

Longs Peak 7½ minute

McHenrys Peak 7½ minute

Larimer County Number Three

Rocky Mountain National Park (available at the entrance)

A beautiful lake, rushing water, and striking rock formations make this a special loop hike using the excellent trails of Rocky Mountain National Park. Remnants of the Fern Lake fire of 2012 are evident en route and around the lake.

Getting There: Enter Rocky Mountain National Park from Estes Park at the Beaver Meadows entrance. After 0.2 mile, turn left on Bear Lake Road. Go 1.3 miles farther and turn right onto Moraine Park Road. It is 1.6 more miles on this road to a parking area at the Cub Lake Trailhead.

The Hike: Begin south and cross Big Thompson River on a bridge. The good trail crosses a meadow and then curves southwest and rises to football field–sized Cub Lake, which is often filled with water lilies. Continue past the lake on the left and ascend to a high point and a trail junction. Take the right fork down another mile to the roaring water at The Pool. Cross the bridge and hike through large rock formations to the Fern Lake Trailhead. Complete this clockwise loop by walking on the road back to the Cub Lake Trailhead.

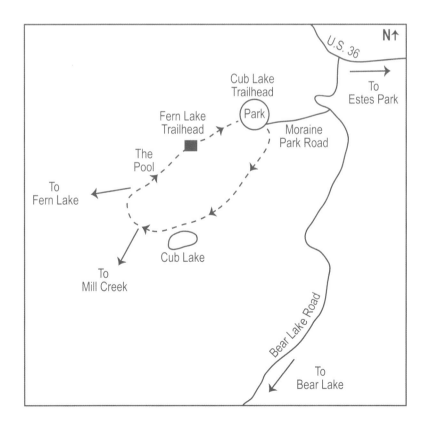

59 Beckwith Pass

Coming down from Beckwith Pass

Hike Distance: 2.6 miles each way

Hiking Time: Up in 67 minutes. Down in 57 minutes.

Starting Elevation: 8,850 feet

Highest Elevation: 9,950 feet

Elevation Gain: 1,470 feet (includes 185 extra feet each way)

Trail: All the way

Relevant Maps: Trails Illustrated 133

   Anthracite Range 7½ minute

   Gunnison County Number Two

   Gunnison Basin Area

B eckwith Pass lies along the northern boundary of the West Elk Wilderness. The Cliff Creek Trail provides the most easterly approach to the pass with many fine vistas along the route. The aspen are dense throughout the first third of the hike. There are a few creek crossings, and in early summer the vegetation is lush. The season for this hike is June until early November.

Getting There: From the bridge at the southwest corner of Crested Butte, drive up Gunnison Road 12 (Kebler Pass Road). Follow this good dirt road 6.9 miles to Kebler Pass and continue west 4.7 more miles. Turn left at the sign for the Cliff Creek Trail and drive 0.2 mile to a parking area and road end at the trailhead.

The Hike: Begin south from the trailhead sign. The trail rises steeply at times, generally to the southwest. Open areas alternate with forested ones on the way. After 2 miles a signed fork is reached. The right trail leads down to Lost Lake Slough in 3 miles. Continue up the left fork (west-southwest) and you will soon pass a series of three spaced wooden poles along the left side of the trail before the final short ascent to signs at the pass, which is named after Lieutenant E.G. Beckwith, an assistant of Captain John W. Gunnison who explored this area. Mount Owen and Ruby Peak can be seen to the north-northeast. East Beckwith Mountain lies to the west and Ohio Peak to the southeast. The trail continues down to the east-southeast toward Swampy Pass and Sheep Lake.

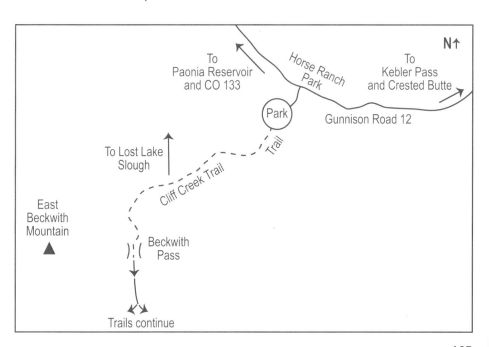

60 Rabbit Ears Peak

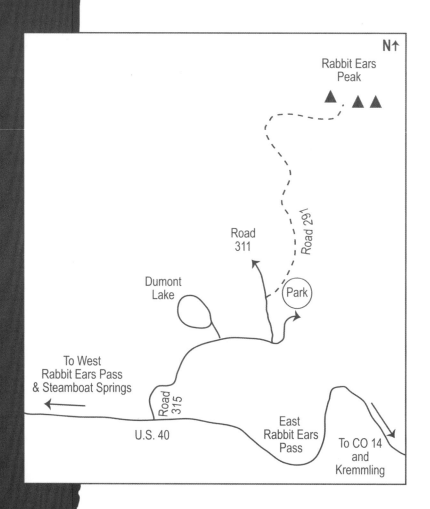

N↑

Rabbit Ears Peak

Road 311

Road 291

Park

Dumont Lake

To West
Rabbit Ears Pass
& Steamboat Springs

Road 315

U.S. 40

East
Rabbit Ears
Pass

To CO 14
and
Kremmling

Rabbit Ears Peak is a sentinel for travelers to the Steamboat Springs area. The volcanic plugs resist the summit hiker but a good road leads to their base and a short trail between the "ears." The route takes you through flower-filled meadows to extensive vistas at the base. Hiking boots are recommended.

Getting There: From U.S. 40 on Rabbit Ears Pass, either drive 6.1 miles east from the western end of the pass or 1.4 miles west from the eastern end. Then go north on Road 315 and set your mileage at zero. After 1.5 miles on this road, turn left at a memorial to old Rabbit Ears Pass and continue on Road 311 0.3 mile farther. Park on the right as Road 291 begins on the right. Regular cars can reach this point but Road 291 requires high clearance and four-wheel drive.

The Hike: Begin on rough Road 291. Follow this main road as it rises and falls through a vast meadow. The way becomes very steep for the final 200 yards up into the trees just below the summit blocks. For the adventurous, a poor trail leads to the right of the large block on the left to a notch between the block and the "ears." Be very careful in this area since the rock is loose and the drop-offs significant. Considerable technical climbing skills would be required to reach the top of these lava towers. Don't try it. Return as you ascended and be especially careful going down the steep 200 yards below the base.

Hike Distance: 2.5 miles each way

Hiking Time: Up in 74 minutes. Down in 64 minutes.

Starting Elevation: 9,590 feet

Highest Elevation: 10,579 feet

Elevation Gain: 1,259 feet (includes 135 extra feet each way)

Trail: All the way

Relevant Maps: Trails Illustrated 118

   Rabbit Ears Peak 7½ minute

   Jackson County Number Three

   Routt National Forest

Views From the Summit: NNW to Mount Ethel

   S to Rabbit Ears Pass

   SSW to Walton Peak

   SE to Whiteley Peak

61 Evergreen Mountain

W ide well-marked trails guide you up to the summit rock of Evergreen Mountain. Lodgepole pine trees line most of the route. Bicycles are allowed and dogs must be on a leash.

Getting There: From the intersection of CO 74 and Jefferson County Road 73 in central Evergreen, drive south on Road 73 for 0.6 mile. Turn right onto Buffalo Park Road and after 2.7 miles, park in the lot on the right at the west trailhead of the park.

The Hike: Begin south-southwest and cross the Buffalo Park Road and go right on the Wild Iris Trail that ascends to a sign and trail junction. Make two right forks here and begin the Evergreen Mountain West Trail that rises one mile to another junction. Ascend the right fork on the Summit Trail for 0.3 mile past a side trail to a scenic view and reach another trail fork. Take the left fork on this final loop. At the highest point on the trail go left and with careful footing ascend the large summit rock to a single tree and a trail register. Enjoy the view and then complete the Summit Loop Trail and return by way of the Evergreen Mountain East Trail, the Ranch View Trail and the eastern half of the Wild Iris Loop.

Hike Distance: 5.7 miles total (two loops)

Hiking Time: Up in 61 minutes. Down in 85 minutes.

Starting Elevation: 7,730 feet

Highest Elevation: 8,536 feet

Elevation Gain: 1,086 feet (includes 280 extra feet)

Trail: All the way

Relevant Maps: Trails Illustrated 100

   Conifer 7½ minute

   Jefferson County Number One

   Alderfer–Three Sisters Park (available at trailhead)

Views From the summit: NW to Squaw Mountain, Bergen Park

   WNW to Chief Mountain

   WSW to Rosalie Peak, Mount Evans

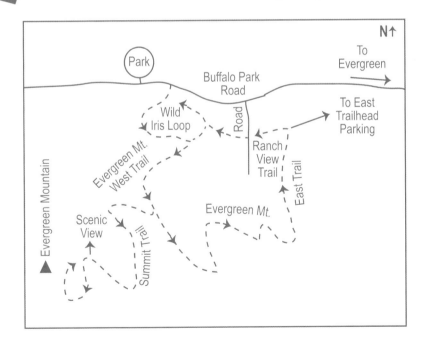

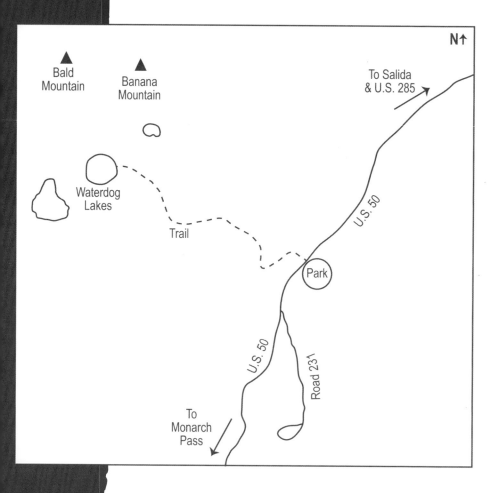

S igns and maps refer to the Waterdog Lakes in the plural. This hike goes to one of them. Located north of Monarch Pass and east of the Continental Divide, this Waterdog Lake is reached by a steep, short trail that begins at the highway. The most difficult aspect of this outing can be locating the obscure trailhead. There are other Colorado lakes with this name.

Getting There: On U.S. 50, either drive west 14.4 miles from its intersection with U.S. 285 north, or east from Monarch Pass for 3.1 miles and park in an open area off the east side of U.S. 50. The trailhead lies opposite at a sign off the west side of the highway.

The Hike: Cross the road and ascend west-northwest into the trees past trail signs and a register. A creek lies to your right. The trail soon bends to the left and leaves the creek. The highway traffic can still be heard as the trail joins an old mining road and sharply rises to the northwest. After 0.25 mile from the trailhead, the grade becomes more level. Continue through evergreen forest and cross the creek at mile 1.3 of your hike. You'll see power poles along the middle third of the trail. The final segment is steeper and passes through a small clearing just before reaching a ridge and a Water-dog Lake sign with the lake just below and straight ahead. A trail leads to a higher Waterdog Lake nearby on the left. The peak to the north-northwest is aptly named, Banana Mountain.

Hike Distance: 2.0 miles each way

Hiking Time: Up in 53 minutes. Down in 36 minutes.

Starting Elevation: 10,360 feet

Highest Elevation: 11,400 feet

Elevation Gain: 1,290 feet (includes 125 extra feet each way)

Trail: All the way

Relevant Maps: Trails Illustrated 130

    Garfield 7½ minute

    Chaffee County Number Three

    San Isabel National Forest

63 | Lulu City

Lulu City flourished between 1879 and 1883 until hopes for mining success were dashed. The population never exceeded 200. Now there are few remnants left of the settlement. The ruins of a few cabins can be found in the flat grassy meadow on the east side of the nascent Colorado River.

Getting There: The Colorado River Trailhead is reached by driving on Trail Ridge Road (U.S. 34) in Rocky Mountain National Park either 10.9 miles south from the Alpine Visitor Center or about 12 miles north from Grand Lake. The paved side road leads northwest 0.1 mile to a parking area at the trailhead.

The Hike: Begin north-northwest from the northwestern end of the parking area. The trail is clear and well-marked as it passes along the eastern banks of the Colorado River. Take the right fork after 0.4 mile from the trailhead and 1.4 miles later pass the Shipler cabin ruins on your right. In 1.1 more miles take a left fork and descend 0.2 mile to the meadow site where Lulu City once stood. Explore the area and maybe have a picnic. This is a good hike for families. The Never Summer Mountain Range lies west of your route to Lulu City and some of its imposing summits may be visible during your hike. (The trail will fork above Lulu City and continue either north to Poudre Pass or northwest to Thunder Pass.)

Hike Distance: 3.1 miles each way

Hiking Time: Up in 82 minutes. Down in 80 minutes.

Starting Elevation: 9,060 feet

Highest Elevation: 9,340 feet

Elevation Gain: 760 feet (includes 190 extra feet each way)

Trail: All the way

Relevant Maps: Trails Illustrated 200

Fall River Pass 7½ minute

Grand County Number Two

Rocky Mountain National Park

Roosevelt National Forest

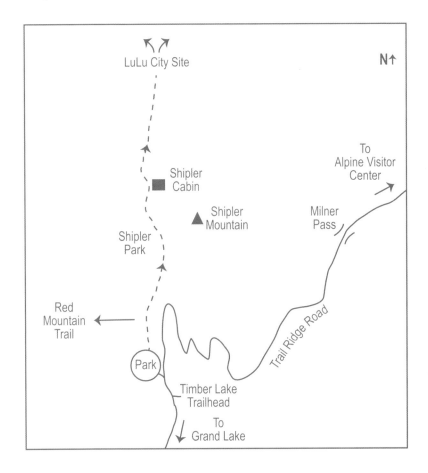

Lower Mohawk Lake and Mohawk Lake

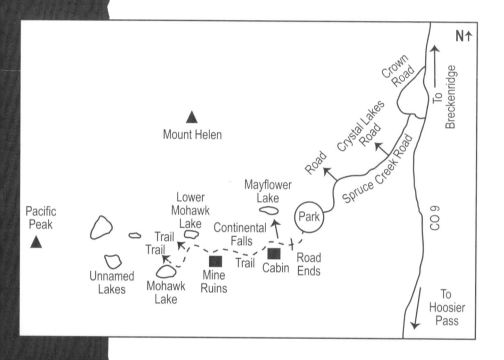

N↑

Crown Road

To Breckenridge

Crystal Lakes Road

Mount Helen

Road

Spruce Creek Road

Mayflower Lake

CO 9

Lower Mohawk Lake

Park

Pacific Peak

Continental Falls

Trail
Trail

Trail

Cabin

Road Ends

Unnamed Lakes

Mohawk Lake

Mine Ruins

To Hoosier Pass

Although somewhat steep, the short hike to the Mohawk Lakes makes a pleasant outing for families. There are many scenic features besides the lakes and peaks. Mining and cabin ruins abound and water rushes near the entire route. There are various side trails on this hike that may be confusing. Stay on the main trail and follow the flowing water of Spruce Creek up to the lakes. The basin above Mohawk Lake to the west contains three un-named lakes below Pacific Peak and Crystal Peak. The gentle mostly trail-less walk to these trees over grassy terrain adds another 1.25 miles to the ascent.

Hike Distance: 1.8 miles each way

Hiking Time: Up in 72 minutes. Down in 60 minutes.

Starting Elevation: 10,980 feet

Highest Elevation: 12,100 feet

Elevation Gain: 1,310 feet (includes 95 extra feet each way)

Trail: All the way

Relevant Maps: Trails Illustrated 109

Breckenridge 7½ minute

Summit County Number Two

Arapaho National Forest—Dillon Ranger District

Getting There: From central Breckenridge drive south on CO 9 from Ski Hill Road for 2.7 miles. Turn right off of CO 9 and ascend Spruce Creek Road for 2.9 miles and park off the road before it becomes steeper and rougher. En route to this point stay on Spruce Creek Road and keep left at mile 0.2, straight at mile 0.5, at mile 0.6 and at mile 0.7 from CO 9. Stay left at mile 1.3 and at mile 2.4. Most regular cars can reach the recommended area to park. Four-wheel drive is required for the final 0.2 mile before the road ends at the Mohawk Lakes Trailhead.

The Hike: Start walking up the rough road to the south and reach the end of the road and a trailhead sign after 0.2 mile. Continue west over 0.3 mile on a steeper trail to a fork. Take the left fork (south). The right fork leads past several cabin ruins to small Mayflower Lake (about 150 yards). You quickly arrive at some mine ruins below two old cabins. Follow the trail to a sign between the cabins and continue south. Soon you will reach an overlook of beautiful Continental Falls to the right. Continue up to a large old mining structure and another 150 yards west-northwest to serene Lower Mohawk Lake with an old cabin on its far shore. Follow the good trail 50 yards along the left side of the lake and take a left fork. After 25 more yards take another left fork and ascend south, with the creek, which flows into Lower Mohawk Lake, on your right. It is another 0.5 mile over good trail to the outlet of Mohawk Lake, which is larger, darker, and more austere than its lower sibling. If time, energy, and weather permit, you may wish to proceed farther west up into the basin. The trail continues upward another 0.25 mile before ending.

65 Fishhook Lake, Lost Lake, and Lake Elmo

This hike uses the Continental Divide Trail, which is also called the Wyoming Trail in this area. The hiker initially descends to an open valley and then gradually ascends to three beautiful lakes lying in the level meadows of the Rabbit Ears Pass area. From Lake Elmo, the highest of these three lakes, the trail continues north to several other lakes and Buffalo Pass.

Getting There: From U.S. 40 on Rabbit Ears Pass, drive north on Road 315, the road to Dumont Lake. This turnoff is 6.2 miles east of West Rabbit Ears Pass and 1.4 miles west of East Rabbit Ears Pass. Follow this paved road 1.5 miles and turn left onto a dirt road at a simple Rabbit Ears Pass Monument. Drive up this road and enter the forest. Keep straight at an intersection after 0.3 mile and follow the main road for 4 more miles to the Base Camp Trailhead and park on the left. Although rough, this road can be negotiated by regular cars with adequate clearance.

The Hike: From the trailhead signs, begin to the northwest and quickly descend over 300 feet through the woods to a meadow and Fishhook Creek. With the Continental Divide always to your right, ascend to the northwest through the trees to reach Fishhook Lake at mile 1.4 from the trailhead. The curve at the northern edge of this very large lake explains its name. Continue by trail along the right side of the lake to a sign at a trail intersection. Take the right fork and reach Lost Lake within 75 yards at mile 1.9 from the trailhead. After visiting Lost Lake, return to the fork and climb to the right for the final 1.1 miles to a vast meadow and Lake Elmo on the left. Relax on the level terrain before retracing your route. Save some energy for the final steep ascent back to the trailhead.

Hike Distance: 3.0 miles each way

Hiking Time: Out in 76 minutes. Back in 76 minutes.

Starting Elevation: 10,040 feet

Highest Elevation: 10,045 feet

Elevation Gain: 1,045 feet (includes 1,040 extra feet)

Trail: All the way

Relevant Maps: Trails Illustrated 118

Mount Werner 7½ minute

Routt County Number Four

Routt National Forest

Fishhook Lake

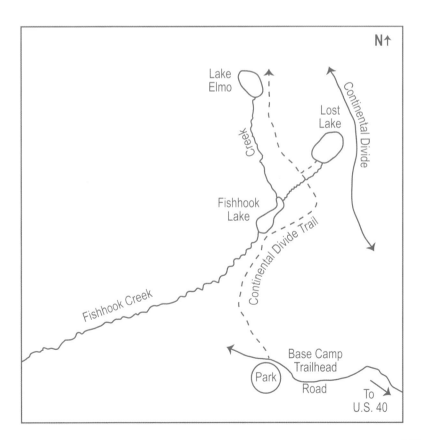

66 Quarry Mountain

Quarry Mountain, called Emerald Mountain by the Steamboat Springs locals, overlooks the town to the west. A wide, unpaved road rises to the foot of the peak near a quarry. A very steep trail then rises almost 500 feet to the summit, where several electronic towers and other artifacts are located. While trees block most of the views

Hike Distance: 2.8 miles each way

Hiking Time: Up in 74 minutes. Down in 56 minutes.

Starting Elevation: 6,760 feet

Highest Elevation: 8,252 feet

Elevation Gain: 1,504 feet (includes 6 extra feet each wa[y]

Trail: All the way

Relevant Maps: Trails Illustrated 118

    Steamboat Springs 7½ minute

    Routt County Number Four

Views From the Summit: N and E to Steamboat Springs

    ENE to Mount Werner

    S to Yampa Valley

from the summit, there are some excellent clear overlooks of Steamboat Springs from segments of the trail on the way down. The trail is popular with local bicyclists.

Getting There: From U.S. 40 (Lincoln Avenue) in Steamboat Springs, drive south on 13th Street for 0.2 mile. Turn left and ascend Gilpin Street. At Saratoga Avenue, turn left and take the first right turn up Routt Street for 1 block and park off-road near a signboard with a blocked dirt road to its right.

The Hike: The trek begins south up the blocked road. Follow this main road upward and never lose elevation. Avoid side trails and keep right at two successive road intersections. Pass the Howelson Hill Ski Area on the left and pass under power lines. There are beautiful meadows and private property to the right off the road. Switchbacks keep the grade reasonable as the road passes occasional cross country ski and bike trail signs. Finally at mile 2.3, the road ends. Take the second trail from the right and ascend steeply around an open green gate. This trail becomes very steep before becoming more level near the top with its busy collection of towers and storage huts.

On your way down, be especially careful on the steep trail segments below the summit. A crisscrossing descent may be helpful. Once you reach the road, it's "clear sailing" back down to the trailhead.

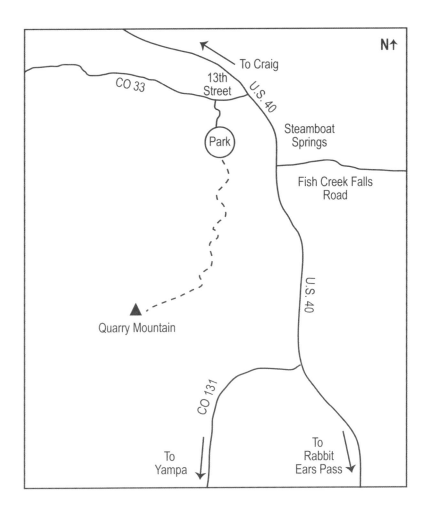

67 Miller Rock

P art one of this outing descends parallel to South Saint Vrain Creek and is especially scenic in the early season. Part two uses rough roads to reach the base of Miller Rock. Part three is a rock scramble to the top with great views of Longs Peak and Indian Peaks.

Getting There: From the stop sign and post office in Jamestown, continue on the paved County Road 94. After 4.3 miles, take the right fork as the paving ends. Take another right fork on the main road after 0.3 mile. Another 0.2 brings you to a sign. Turn right and park in another 0.1 mile.

The Hike: Descend northeast, quickly passing a sign about Saint Vrain and cross a bridge. With South Saint Vrain Creek always on the right, go down 2 miles to a rough road. This is the lowest point of the hike. Continue left on Road 252. After 0.25 mile, pass a trail on the left and continue straight (west). After a steep uphill segment, pass a 4-way intersection with trail number signs. Continue straight on Road 252 down 60 yards and ascend left on Road 252A. Soon go right at a T junction and prominent Miller Rock comes into view. Avoid another side road on the left and rise to the base of Miller Rock. Of the several routes to the top, I prefer passing around to the right and using some easy handwork to reach the bare, unmarked summit and great viewing.

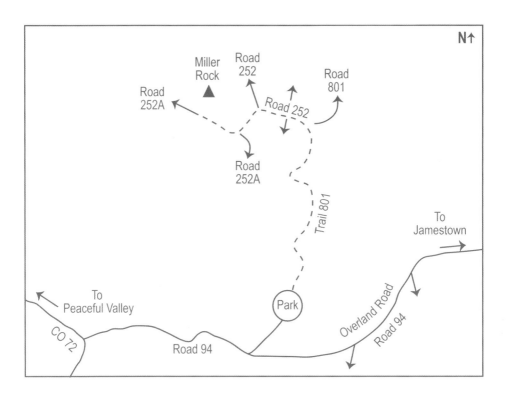

Hike Distance: 3.2 miles total

Hiking Time: Up in 82 minutes. Down in 80 minutes.

Starting Elevation: 8,330 feet

Highest Elevation: 8,646 feet

Lowest Elevation: 7,960 feet

Elevation Gain: 1,256 feet (includes 570 extra feet)

Trail: All the way

Relevant Maps: Trails Illustrated 102

    Raymond 7½ minute

    Gold Hill 7½ minute

    Boulder County

    Roosevelt National Forest

Views From the summit: NW to Ypsilon Mountin, Estes Cone

    W to Pagoda Mountain

    WNW to Longs Peak

    WSW to Saint Vrain Mountain

68 Peak 12,479

This is a short hike on the Continental Divide to an unnamed peak with a terrific 360-degree set of vistas.

Getting There: Take U.S. 6 to Loveland Pass between I-70 on the east and Keystone on the west. Park on the east side of the pass.

The Hike: Start out west from the pass and follow the good trail as it winds up the Continental Divide past a subpeak and cairn. Your route goes from southwest, west, and northwest to the flat unmarked summit with a wind shelter on the left and a large cairn on the right. Enjoy the great scenery.

Hike Distance: 2.0 miles each way

Hiking Time: Up in 48 minutes. Down in 37 minutes.

Starting Elevation: 11,990 feet (Loveland Pass)

Highest Elevation: 12,479 feet

Elevation Gain: 739 feet (includes 125 extra feet each way)

Trail: All the way

Relevant Maps: Trails Illustrated 104

Loveland Pass 7½ minute

Clear Creek County

Arapaho National Forest

Views From the Summit: N to Mount Bethel

NNW to Hagar Peak, Pettingell Peak, Mount Trelease

NE to Mount Sniktau

E to Torreys Peak

ESE to Grays Peak, Grizzly Peak

View of Peak 12,479

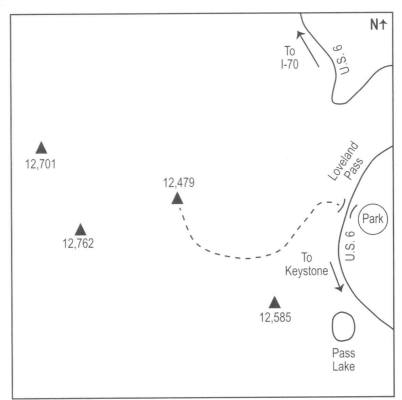

Grays Lake

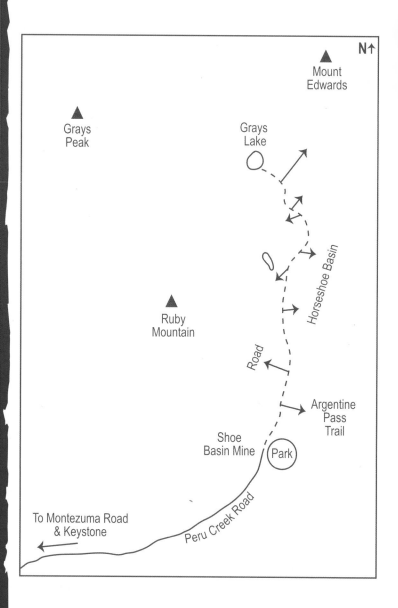

N↑

Mount
Edwards

Grays
Peak

Grays
Lake

Horseshoe Basin

Ruby
Mountain

Road

Argentine
Pass
Trail

Shoe
Basin Mine

Park

To Montezuma Road
& Keystone

Peru Creek Road

Little Grays Lake is located below the southern flanks of Grays Peak and is seldom visited. High in Horseshoe Basin with its numerous mine remnants, the small, high lake is ringed by impressive peaks. The hiking route uses a rough road for most of the way.

Getting There:
From I-70 at Dillon and Silverthorne, take Exit 205 and go east on U.S. 6 for 7.8 miles. Turn right onto Montezuma Road. This turn is 100 yards past the entrance to the Keystone Ski Area. Follow Montezuma Road for 4.7 miles and turn left onto Peru Creek Road. Follow the main, unpaved, Peru Creek Road up the valley for 4.6 miles and park on the right near a cabin ruin with the old Shoe Basin Mine on the left. On Peru Creek Road, keep left at mile 1.1 and at mile 3.7 en route to the parking area. Regular cars can reach the parking area.

Hike Distance: 2.4 miles each way

Hiking Time: Up in 76 minutes.
Down in 54 minutes.

Starting Elevation: 11,100 feet

Highest Elevation: 12,475 feet

Elevation Gain: 1,440 feet (includes 65 extra feet)

Trail: Initial 2.2 miles

Relevant Maps: Trails Illustrated 104

Grays Peak 7½ minute

Montezuma 7½ minute

Summit County Number Two

Arapaho National Forest—Dillon Ranger District

The Hike: Start on foot up the road to the north. The road becomes considerably rougher as you pass the Argentine Pass Trail on the right at 0.3 mile. Continue along the main road and take a right fork after another 0.1 mile. At mile 0.7, take the left fork and 0.2 mile farther, take the route on the right. You will soon go left and then right at successive forks up to a cabin ruin. The lake below is unnamed. Here you leave the road and follow a cairn-marked trail to the west and up to a grassy bench. Then leave the trail and proceed to the west-northwest in the direction of the Grays Peak summit hovering above. Within 150 yards, you will reach small Grays Lake lying below a rocky bluff. This clear lake is only about 40 yards long and 40 yards wide. Argentine Pass can be seen to the east and Argentine Peak to the east-southeast. Ruby Mountain impresses to the south-southeast. Unless you want to continue up to Grays Peak, return as you ascended through vast Horseshoe Basin.

70 | Fourmile Falls

I f possible, plan this outing when water levels are high in order
to get the full effect of the falls. Lying in the Weminuche Wilderness, the trail continues another 3 miles up to Fourmile Lake,
which is considerably farther from the trailhead than four miles.

Getting There: From Highway 160 in central Pagosa
Springs drive north on Fifth Street and then onto Fourmile
Road, for a total of 13 miles to the Fourmile Lake Trailhead at
the end of the road.

The Hike: Begin on the right fork from the trailhead register and signboard. Lose some elevation before the trail begins
to rise. Eagle Mountain can be seen on the right. Pass eventually
through a clearing and the falls will be above on the left. Enjoy
the rushing water.

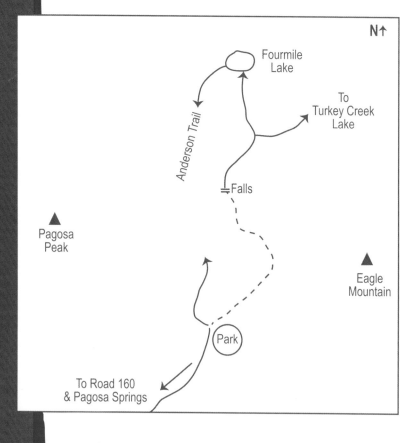

Author, Diane Gimber, and Frank Beghtel at Fourmile Falls

Hike Distance: 3.3 miles each way

Hiking Time: Up in 85 minutes. Down in 62 minutes.

Starting Elevation: 9,040 feet

Highest Elevation: 9,600 feet

Elevation Gain: 660 feet (includes 50 extra feet each way)

Trail: All the way

Relevant Maps: Trails Illustrated 140

    Pagosa Peak 7½ minute

    Mineral County

    San Juan National Forest

71 Red Rocks—Dakota Ridge Loop

Red Rocks Theatre from the Dakota Ridge Trail

Hike Distance: Out in 3.1 miles (Red Rocks Trail). Back in 2.8 miles (Dakota Ridge Trail).

Hiking Time: Out in 75 minutes. Back in 90 minutes.

Starting Elevation: 6,360 feet

Lowest Elevation: 5,990 feet

Highest Elevation: 6,620 feet

Elevation Gain: 1,450 feet (includes 820 extra feet)

Trail: All the way

Relevant Maps: Trails Illustrated 100

Morrison 7½ minute

Jefferson County Number One

Matthews/Winters Park Map (available at trailhead)

This loop hike lies close to metropolitan Denver and can usually be hiked from April through November. The first half takes you down a valley from the old town site of Mount Vernon and past red rock formations. The return is on the Dakota Ridge, part of the hogback between CO 26 and C-470. There are nice vistas from the ridge and some informational signs.

Getting There: From I-70 west of Denver, drive to the Morrison–Red Rocks Exit 259 and drive south on CO 26 for 100 yards and turn right into the Matthews/Winters parking lot at the trailhead.

The Hike: Start out to the south on the Village Walk Trail. Cross over a creek, ascend a ridge, and take the right (south-southeast) fork and continue down the valley on the main trail. Another .75 mile brings you to a junction with the Morrison Slide Trail. Keep left and stay on the Red Rocks Trail. In 0.8 mile the trail descends sharply to the right and reaches a signed fork amid the red rocks. Descend to the left and soon cross a road and follow the trail signs, which lead you over another dirt road and down to a paved road. This is the southern end of the Red Rocks Trail. You have hiked 3.1 miles. Red Rocks Park is visible to the southwest. Continue down the road to the left (northeast) and cross CO 26. To the right is the sign for the Dakota Ridge Trail. Proceed north on this trail, which rises to the ridge, and then descends to a paved road and geologic informational signs on the right. Hike down along the right side of the road 50 yards and cross the road on the left. Then ascend a series of high points along the Dakota Ridge and enjoy the vistas. Stay on or close to the ridge, avoid the Zorro Trail on the right, and reach the highest point before descending the trail, which passes the Stegosaurus parking area on the right and ends at CO 26. Cross the road and return to your starting point at Matthews/Winters Park.

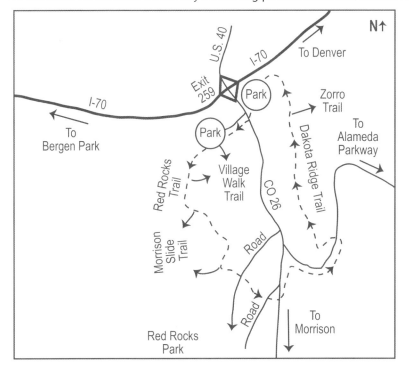

72 Columbine Lake

Hike Distance: 2.9 miles each way

Hiking Time: Up in 80 minutes. Down in 65 minutes.

Starting Elevation: 10,046 feet

Highest Elevation: 11,090 feet

Elevation Gain: 1,534 feet (includes 490 extra feet)

Trail: All the way

Relevant Maps: Trails Illustrated 102

Monarch Lake 7½ minute

Grand County Number Four

Arapaho National Forest

The relatively short hike to lovely Columbine Lake in the Indian Peaks Wilderness rewards with flowing water, lush meadows, and surrounding rocky peaks. The trail is adequate. The greatest challenge of this outing is to take the proper turns on the road from U.S. 40 to the trailhead. Snow lingers around the lake through June. The middle of July would be ideal.

Getting There: From the stop light in central Fraser, drive northwest on U.S. 40 for 3 miles and turn right onto Grand County Road 83. All distances given will be from U.S. 40. After 0.4 mile go left on Grand County Road 84. Keep right at mile 1.2 and left at mile 1.3. Stay on the main road as it ascends to Meadow Creek Reservoir. Keep left at mile 2.6 and at mile 6.2. Take the right fork at mile 7. Meadow Creek Reservoir will soon be on your right. Continue on the main road and turn left at mile 8.8 and go right at mile 9.7. Keep straight twice at mile 10.8 and then left at mile 11.1 at a sign. After 0.3 mile farther, park at the large Junco Lake Trailhead. Regular cars can reach this point.

The Hike: From the parking area, begin east at the trailhead signboard. Avoid the High Lonesome Trail, which runs north to south. Follow the wide road that eventually narrows to a trail. Pass a cabin ruin on the right and then a wilderness sign. After 1.5 miles from the trailhead keep right at the signed fork. The left trail rises to Caribou Pass. Continue along the valley floor with Meadow Creek on your right. At several places the trail forks, but both trails then reunite. When in doubt, take the clearer trail and follow the creek up to the lake. After a creek crossing, the last 0.5 mile gets steeper and more rocky before your final level approach to this gorgeous lake. Mount Neva is the impressive peak to the southeast. Enjoy your scenic surroundings and relax before returning, as you came, to the parking area.

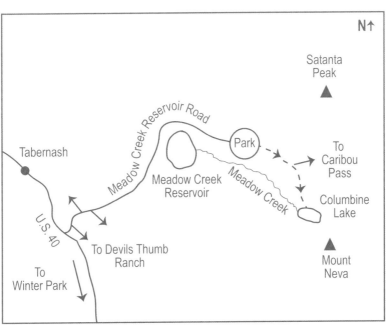

153

Shrine Mountain

Hike Distance: 2.2 miles each way

Hiking Time: Up in 58 minutes. Down in 48 minutes.

Starting Elevation: 11,089 feet

Highest Elevation: 11,888 feet

Elevation Gain: 919 feet (includes 60 extra feet each way)

Trail: All the way

Relevant Maps: Trails Illustrated 108 or 149

Vail Pass 7½ minute

Red Cliff 7½ minute

Summit County Number Two

Eagle County Number Four

Arapaho and White River National Forests

Views From the Summit: NNE to the "Shrine"

NNW to Mount Powell

NE to Shrine Mountain Inn and Shrine Pass

ENE to Uneva Peak, Peak One and Peak Two

ESE to Pacific Peak

S to Mount Massive

SSE to Ptarmigan Hill and Mount Elbert

SE to Jaque Peak

SW to Mount of the Holy Cross

N amed after the prominent rock formation 100 yards to the north, Shrine Mountain is an easy, popular and rewarding hike destination. The easy walk begins near Shrine Pass, a popular cross-country ski area in the winter. Nearby Shrine Mountain Inn offers high country lunch and dinner in the summer, and overnight accommodations for Nordic skiers in the colder months.

Getting There: From I-70 east of Vail Pass, take Exit 190 and drive south 0.1 mile and take a right fork onto the unpaved Shrine Pass Road. Follow this good, wide road 2.4 miles to a White River National Forest sign, and a road on the left. Park in the adjacent parking area. Regular cars can reach this point.

The Hike: From the parking area, walk southwest up the side road. After 0.25 mile take the right fork and quickly reach a sign on the left. Shrine Mountain Inn lies straight ahead within 50 yards. Turn left here onto the well-demarcated Shrine Ridge Trail and proceed to the south-southwest over a boardwalk. The trail continues up through lush, semi-open meadow and bends to the right (west-northwest) before passing large red boulders on the left. Ascend to the ridge where a pole embedded in the rocks marks the trail. At the ridge, turn right on either of two trails which lead north to the summit of Shrine Mountain. Two benchmarks signify the high point. The view from here can be breathtaking. The Gore Range, the Tenmile Range, and many high peaks to the west can be seen. Savor it and return as you came. Halfway back to the trailhead, take a left fork and stay in the meadow in retracing your route.

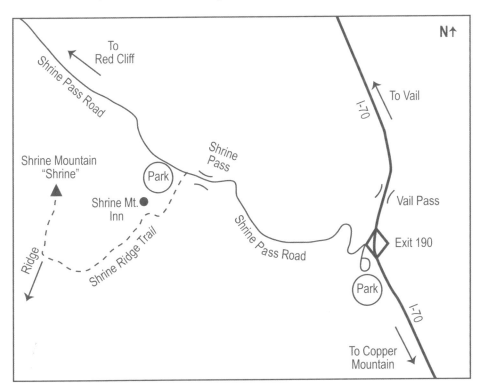

Hike Distance: 2.4 miles each way

Hiking Time: Up in 68 minutes. Down in 66 minutes.

Starting Elevation: 10,180 feet

Highest Elevation: 10,950 feet

Elevation Gain: 1,550 feet (includes 780 extra feet)

Trail: All the way

Relevant Maps: Trails Illustrated 102

East Portal 7½ minute

Monarch Lake 7½ minute

Boulder County

Roosevelt National Forest

Diamond Lake and South Arapaho Peak

Any hike in the Indian Peaks Wilderness is a winner. The trail from Bucking-ham Campground is very popular and the parking areas are usually crowded. Arapaho Pass and South Arapaho Peak are other destinations that can be reached from this trailhead. The rushing waters of Middle Boulder Creek enhance this hike to a lovely lake.

Getting There: From the intersection of CO 119 and CO 72 in Nederland, drive south on CO 119 for 0.6 mile and turn right onto Boulder Road 130. Turn your mileage to zero. Keep right at mile 0.8 and again at mile 1.9. Drive through the town of Eldora and up the unpaved road beyond. Keep right at mile 4.1 and continue up the right fork to parking and end of road at mile 8.2.

The Hike: Begin to the north from the trailhead signs at the upper parking area. The good trail curves west with intermittent vistas as it climbs to a signed fork at mile 1.3. Take the left fork to the west, as the other trail ascends up the valley toward Arapaho Pass. Gradually descend into the thick forest for 0.7 mile to a crossing of the north fork of Middle Boulder Creek on a bridge. A scenic waterfall can be viewed 50 yards upstream. Continue the final 0.6 mile up to a signed trail fork in a clearing. Go right (south) 100 yards to the diamond-shaped lake with several nearby camp-sites. The Continental Divide lies to the west and towering South Arapaho Peak can be seen through the trees to the north-northwest.

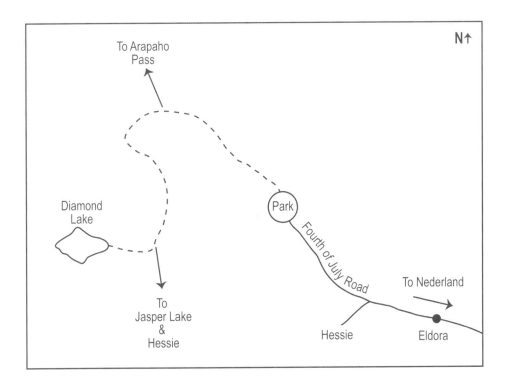

75 Legault Mountain

View south from Legault Mountain with Baldy Peak in the distance

This good early or late-season hike utilizes Meyer Ranch Park, one of the excellent Jefferson County parks. No fee is required. There are maps at the trailhead and picnic and toilet facilities are available. The park lies less than 30 miles from downtown Denver. The route ascends well-marked trails and then requires some easy bushwhacking (hiking by compass without a trail) for the final 0.7 mile up to a good overlook from the small, rocky summit.

Getting There: Drive on U.S. 285 to the junction with South Turkey Creek Road (just east of Aspen Park). Turn left onto South Turkey Creek Road and park on the right within 75 yards of U.S. 285.

The Hike: Begin south on the Owls Perch Trail and after 150 yards take a right fork at a trail with a picnic table sign. Ascend a left fork, bypass a picnic table and pass a water pump. After 0.7 mile from the trailhead, continue left on the Lodgepole Trail. In 0.2 mile go left on the Sunny Aspen Trail, which ascends 0.5 mile to a covered picnic table at a fork. Here, you go left and ascend the Old Ski Run Trail, which leads to a terminal trail loop in 0.75 mile. Take the left fork, which soon passes a rocky area above to the left. Avoid this overlook and continue to ascend another 0.2 mile to a place where you will leave the trail. There is an open meadow on the left (southeast) with some park boundary signs nearby. A faint side trail leads southeast, but you avoid this and ascend due east past the park boundary, through the sparse forest. Pass between some rocky areas and ascend an easy 0.7 mile from the loop trail to the top of Legault Mountain, which is marked by two benchmarks and a wooden pole fixed in a rock pile. The views are quite good from here. Descend to the west and find your way back to the Old Ski Run Trail and continue the loop back to the last trail fork. Go left here and retrace your ascent route back to the trailhead unless you wish to go left at three forks and try the other halves of the three lower loop trails.

Hike Distance: 6.0 miles (total, includes upper loop)

Hiking Time: Up in 75 minutes. Down in 55 minutes.

Starting Elevation: 7,830 feet

Highest Elevation: 9,074 feet

Elevation Gain: 1,414 feet (includes 170 extra feet)

Trail: All but the final 0.7 mile en route to summit

Relevant Maps: Trails Illustrated 100

   Conifer 7½ minute

   Meyer Ranch Park (Jefferson County Open Space)

   Jefferson County Number Two

   Pike National Forest

Views From the Summit: N to Doublehead Mountain

   NE to downtown Denver

   W to Mount Evans

   WNW to Chief Mountain and Squaw Mountain

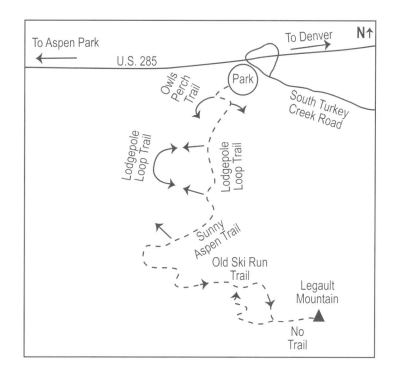

76 Paines Mountain

Leavenworth Gulch Road, southwest of Georgetown, provides access to many good hiking targets. Most of these lie higher in the basin and west of the road. Paines Mountain, however, lies to the east of Leavenworth Road and is rarely visited by hikers. Reaching its unmarked summit requires some good route-finding and map-reading.

Getting There: From the intersection at Rose Street in central Georgetown, drive south up Sixth Street, which becomes

Hike Distance: 2.1 miles each way

Hiking Time: Up in 65 minutes. Down in 42 minutes.

Starting Elevation: 10,870 feet

Highest Elevation: 12,048 feet

Elevation Gain: 1,208 feet (includes 15 extra feet each wa

Trail: Initial two-thirds

Relevant Maps: Trails Illustrated 104

Georgetown 7½ minute

Clear Creek County

Arapaho National Forest

Views From the Summit: N to James Peak

E to Sugarloaf Mountain

SSE to Otter Mountain

SSW to Square Top Mountain and Mount Wilcox

SW to Argentine Peak

SE to Mount Evans and Mount Bierstadt

WNW to Ganley Mountain and Pendleton Mountain

Guanella Pass Road. Follow this paved road for 2.7 miles from Rose Street. As the road curves sharply left, leave the road and set your mileage to zero at the beginning of the rough road on the right to the old Waldorf Mine site. Ascend this road and keep right after 0.25 mile. Stay left at mile 0.4 and take the right fork at mile 1.0. At mile 1.2, curve sharply left. You are now on Leavenworth Gulch Road. Follow this gradual road up the valley to a fork at mile 3.5. Here you descend left. Take the right fork at mile 3.7. Pass some mine remnants before taking a left fork at mile 4.2. Descend less than 100 yards under power lines and park off-road just before Leavenworth Creek. Some cars with good clearance might be able to reach this point, but a four-wheel drive vehicle would be preferable from Guanella Pass Road.

The Hike: From Leavenworth Creek, begin east up the dirt road. Avoid a road on the right within 200 yards and take a right fork after 0.3 mile from Leavenworth

Creek. Continue up another 0.6 mile and take the road on the right. In 0.2 mile more, reach a road junction and go left (north) on Road 248.1E. Another ascending 0.3 mile brings you to the end of the road. Then continue up west-northwest into the forest and gradually angle to the left, and always be gaining altitude. Carefully mark and remember your way. About 0.3 mile of bushwhacking will bring you to tree line and grassy slopes above. From here, angle east-southeast to the unmarked rocky knob atop Paines Mountain. Consult the map since Paines Mountain is not the highest nearby point on this ridge. It is the northernmost peak above 12,000 feet. From its summit, the ridge descends north about 300 feet to the next saddle on the ridge. Many identifiable mountains can be seen from the high point. Be sure of your direction in the bushwhack back down to the road you ascended.

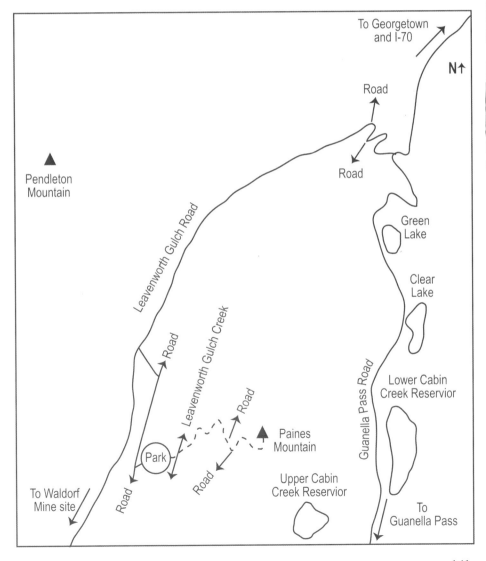

77 Bierstadt Lake from Hollowell Park

Hike Distance: 3.1 miles each way

Hiking Time: Up in 82 minutes. Down in 67 minutes.

Starting Elevation: 8,320 feet

Highest Elevation: 9,520 feet

Elevation Gain: 1,355 feet (includes 155 extra feet)

Trail: All the way

Relevant Maps: Trails Illustrated 200 or 301

Longs Peak 7½ minute

McHenrys Peak 7½ minute

Larimer County Number Three

Rocky Mountain National Park (available at entrance)

There are three main trails to Bierstadt Lake. All leave Bear Lake Road. This one starts at Hollowell Park and follows Mill Creek part of the way before leaving the creek and reaching scenic Bierstadt Lake, which empties into Mill Creek. As with all the trails in Rocky Mountain National Park, the route is clear and there are signs at most junctions. Late May and early June are recommended if you enjoy flowing water.

Getting There: From the Beaver Meadows entrance to Rocky Mountain National Park (fee required), drive west into the park for 0.2 mile, turn left on the Bear Lake Road and set your mileage to zero. Then drive 3.5 miles on the Bear Lake Road and turn right into Hollowell Park and after 0.2 mile, park at the Mill Creek Trailhead.

The Hike: From the parking area and the trailhead signboard, begin to the west-southwest through a large meadow. Keep left at an early fork and enter the forest with Mill Creek on your left. Ascend gradually with Steep Mountain above on your right. At the 1-mile mark, keep left at a fork across Mill Creek on a bridge. Another 0.7 mile brings you to a trail junction and a sign. The trail on the right leads to Cub Lake in 1.9 miles. You continue straight another 0.2 mile and take a left fork (southeast) as you leave Mill Creek. Follow the good signs through the woods to a high point at mile 2.6 of your hike. Descend gently to another signed fork and go left (east) the final 0.3 mile to beautiful Bierstadt Lake. On a clear day, the mountains to the south are striking. Longs Peak is south-southeast and Hallett Peak and Flattop Mountain lie to the southwest. Drink in this visual beauty before retracing your 3.1 mile route back to Hollowell Park.

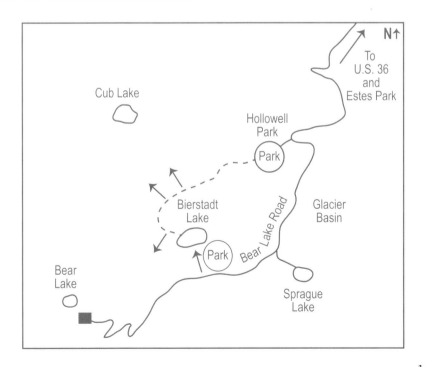

78 Mills Lake and Jewel Lake

Hike Distance: 3.0 miles each way

Hiking Time: Up in 70 minutes.
Down in 60 minutes.

Starting Elevation: 9,210 feet

Highest Elevation: 9,950 feet

Elevation Gain: 1,450 feet (includes 355 extra feet each way)

Trail: All the way

Relevant Maps: Trails Illustrated 200 or 301

McHenrys Peak 7½ minute

Larimer County Number Three

Rocky Mountain National Park

Trails from Glacier Gorge Junction and Bear Lake in Rocky Mountain National Park are very popular. To avoid the crowds, try weekdays, off-season, or even at off hours. An entrance fee is required and bikes, weapons, and pets are forbidden on the trails. The scenic grandeur and the superb trails are invariably rewarding. Mills Glacier, Lake, and Moraine are named after Enos Mills, an outdoorsman and naturalist who promoted the establishment of Rocky Mountain National Park in the early 1900s.

Getting There: From the Beaver Meadows Entrance Station to Rocky Mountain National Park (west of Estes Park), drive into the park for 0.2 mile and turn left onto Bear Lake Road. Follow this paved road for 8.7 miles and park in the Glacier Gorge parking area. (If this lot is full, try the huge Bear Lake lot farther up the road.)

The Hike: Begin south/southwest from the trailhead signboard. After 0.3 mile, pass a trail on the left to Sprague Lake. Ascend 35 yards more to a T intersection with signs. Go left, which will take you to the scenic Mills and Jewel Lakes after 5 bridge crossings. After 0.6 mile on the excellent trail, pass an overlook of Alberta Falls on the left. Continue up another 0.8 mile to a signed fork. The trail on the left leads to Granite Pass and beyond. You ascend to the right (southeast) for another 0.5 mile to a four-way intersection and signs. Straight leads to Loch Vale and right continues to Lake Haiyaha. You proceed to the left and rise more steeply over some rocky terrain the last 0.6 mile to lovely Mills Lake. The impressive peaks up the valley are from left to right: Longs Peak, Pagoda Mountain, and Chiefs Head Peak. The trail continues another 0.5 mile up the valley to smaller Jewel Lake, which empties into Mills Lake. Another 2.2 miles up the valley lies Black Lake and more visual treats.

Mills Lake

Bear Lake

To Estes Park

Bear Lake Road

Park

Lake Haiyaha

Alberta Falls

To Granite Pass

Mills Lake

The Loch

Jewel Lake

To Black Lake

Storm Peak

Black Lake

N↑

79 | Mount Chapin

F all River Road is one of the many treasures of Rocky Mountain
National Park. The rushing waters of Fall River can be seen on
the left as you ascend this one-way road up a steep canyon to
connect with Trail Ridge Road. The road is open from late June
until October. Regular cars can traverse this excellent dirt road.
A descriptive booklet with information about the Fall River Road
can be purchased at park visitor centers. Mount Chapin is the most
southerly and lowest peak of the Mummy Range.

Getting There: From the northwestern edge of Estes Park,
enter Rocky Mountain National Park by the Fall River entrance and
drive 2.1 miles west on U.S. 34. Then turn right into Horseshoe
Park. Follow this road up the valley where it becomes Fall River
Road, which is a good one-way dirt road leading up to the Alpine
Visitor Center at Fall River Pass and Trail Ridge Road. Ascend scenic
Fall River Road for 8.6 miles from U.S. 34 and park off of the road
on the left at the Chapin Pass Trailhead, which is on the right side
of the road.

The Hike: Begin steeply to the north from the trailhead sign.
In a few hundred yards, reach unmarked Chapin Pass at 11,150
feet. Take a right fork here at a sign that describes the Mount
Chapin Trail. Continue southeast and eventually pass a small tarn
on your right just below timberline. Take a right fork just past the
tarn and ascend the trail to the east past the last trees. The green
rounded hill to the north is a false summit of Mount Chapin.
Continue heading east toward the right side of the saddle between
Mount Chiquita and Mount Chapin. Do not lose any elevation and
keep your ascent gradual as the trail ends and you walk over tundra
and some talus to a cairn and a few rock shelters atop Mount
Chapin. Enjoy the magnificent views in every direction. A false
summit can be seen to the southwest. An option from this point is
to walk the ridge to the northeast to Mount Chiquita and Mount
Ypsilon, both over 13,000 feet. Return by generally retracing your
ascent route back to the trail.

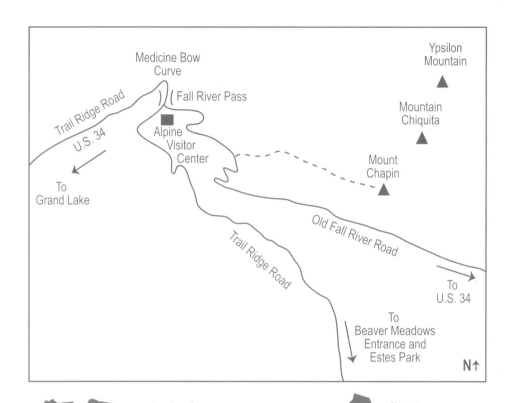

Hike Distance: 1.8 miles each way

Hiking Time: Up in 65 minutes. Down in 55 minutes.

Starting Elevation: 11,025 feet

Highest Elevation: 12,454 feet

Elevation Gain: 1,489 feet (includes 30 extra feet each way)

Trail: First half

Relevant Maps: Trails Illustrated 200

Trail Ridge 7½ minute

Larimer County Number Three

Rocky Mountain National Park

Views From the Summit: NNE to Hagues Peak

NE to Mount Chiquita

NW to Clark Peak

SSE to McHenrys Peak

SE to Twin Sisters Peaks, the Estes Cone, Mount Meeker, Longs Peak, Pagoda Mountain, and Chiefs Head Peak

W to Mount Richthofen

80 Twining Peak

Located on the Continental Divide, this mountain forms part of the boundary between Pitkin and Lake Counties and the White River and San Isabel National Forests.

Getting There: Drive to Independence Pass on paved CO 82 west from Twin Lakes or east from Aspen. Park in the large paved area at the pass.

The Hike: Proceed from the east side of the road on a trail that passes along the right side of a small pond at the pass. Continue north on this faint trail as it rises toward the ridge and then disappears. Keep to the left of the rocky ridge and cross the tundra to a group of boulders at the summit. Some easy hand work may be needed to reach a boulder with a small cairn at the high point. Return directly south to Independence Pass.

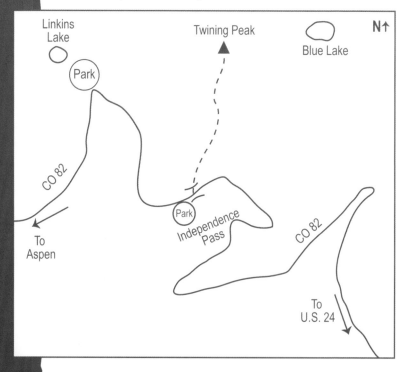

Twining Peak from Independence Pass

Hike Distance: 2.0 miles each way

Hiking Time: Up in 57 minutes. Down in 35 minutes.

Starting Elevation: 12,095 feet (Independence Pass)

Elevation Gain: 1,616 feet

Trail: Initial 35%

Relevant Maps: Trails Illustrated 127

    Mount Champion 7½ minute

    Independence Pass 7½ minute

    Pitkin County Number One

    White River National Forest

Views From the Summit: NE to Mount Elbert, Deer Mountain, and Mount Champion

    NW to Geissler Mountain and Independence Lake

    S to Grizzly Peak

    SE to La Plata Peak

    WSW to Linkins Lake

81 Oliver Twist Lake and Cooney Lake

The area between Fairplay and Leadville is full of old mines and mining settlements. Mosquito Pass Road connects these two towns by a four-wheel-drive road, which provides access to many of the remnants of the gold rush in the last two decades of the nineteenth century. This hike to two high lakes is totally above timberline and uses Mosquito Pass Road from the Fairplay side. You can reach the trailhead without four-wheel drive. Then ascend easily past mine ruins and end in a basin with peaks of the Mosquito Range to the west.

Getting There: Drive north from Fairplay on CO 9 from its intersection with U.S. 285 4.6 miles and turn left onto Park County Road Number 12. This is Mosquito Pass Road, which is marked by a series of wagon wheel signs every mile. Follow this dirt road and take right forks at mile 4.4, mile 5.5, and mile 6.2. At mile 6.7, take a sharp left fork and park at mile 6.8 near a sign that gives some information about Mosquito Pass Road. Regular cars can come this far, but four-wheel drive and high clearance are required above and beyond this point.

The Hike: Begin south on Mosquito Pass Road from the historical sign. After 0.75 mile on this rough road, take a right fork off the main road. Then proceed west-northwest on a more primitive dirt road and soon reach Oliver Twist Lake with mine ruins on its southern edge. Follow the road with the lake on your left. Soon take a left fork and ascend counterclockwise 1.25 miles from Oliver Twist Lake to reach Cooney Lake. This lake lies in a basin with Treasurevault Mountain to the west and Mosquito Peak to the southwest. Be careful of the open mining pits in the area. Return as you ascended.

Hike Distance: 2.3 miles each way

Hiking Time: Up in 56 minutes. Down in 46 minutes.

Starting Elevation: 12,190 feet

Highest Elevation: 12,580 feet

Elevation Gain: 570 feet (includes 90 extra feet each way)

Trail: All the way

Relevant Maps: Trails Illustrated 109, 110, or 149

    Climax 7½ minute

    Park County Number One

    Pike National Forest

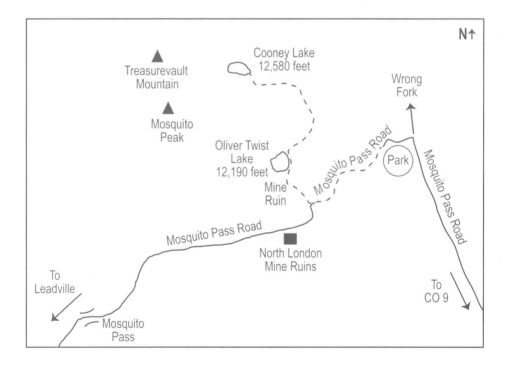

Crater Lakes Overlook

82

Crater Lakes from the Continental Divide

Hike Distance: 2.5 miles each way

Hiking Time: Up in 90 minutes. Down in 67 minutes.

Starting Elevation: 11,671 feet

Highest Elevation: 12,038 feet

Elevation Gain: 742 feet (includes 375 extra feet)

Trail: All the way to the final 100 feet

Relevant Maps: Trails Illustrated 103

    East Portal 7½ minute

    Grand County Number Four

    Arapaho National Forest

Rollins Pass is a former train route. The site around the pass once had a hotel and was called Corona. Following the Continental Divide Trail over tundra, you reach several overlooks to the east and many lakes.

Getting There: From U.S. 40 at the south side of Winter Park 11.8 miles south of Berthoud Pass, or 1.7 miles north of Vasquez Road, drive northeast on the unpaved Rollins Pass Road (also called the Moffat Road). Follow this road, designated Road 149, 13.8 miles and park at the Rollins Pass sign. Regular cars with good clearance can reach this trailhead.

The Hike: Start out southeast, cross the road and follow a series of wooden poles that lead to the south. Along the way, the ridge on the left offers great overlooks. The first valley contains the Forest Lakes and the second contains the Arapaho Lakes. The overlook of the third valley reveals the four Crater Lakes and is the terminus of this outing. Over the last 0.25 mile the poles are replaced by a faint trail. James Peak is visible to the south and Mount Epworth to the north-northwest.

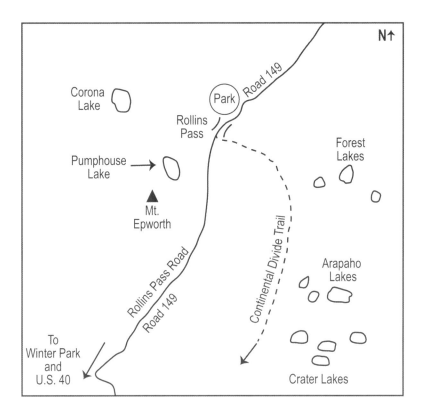

83 | Lake Helene

All trails in Rocky Mountain National Park are well marked and scenic. Pets and vehicles are forbidden on the trails. The park is especially crowded on weekends and holidays. This is one of several trails that begin at very popular Bear Lake.

Getting There: From Estes Park, enter Rocky Mountain National Park on the eastern side by the Beaver Meadows Entrance. An entry fee is required and a map is provided. After 0.2 mile, turn left onto Bear Lake Road and drive to the Bear Lake parking area.

The Hike: Begin to the west around the right side of Bear Lake. Within 300 yards, take the right fork and ascend more steeply. Avoid a horse trail on the right. Soon take a left at a signed fork. After another 0.5 mile, take a right fork. Soon pass a trail to Sourdough Campground on the right and descend to an unmarked fork as the main trail descends right to Odessa and Fern Lakes. Take the left fork a few hundred yards to reach Lake Helene with the striking Odessa Gorge above to the right. Notchtop is impressive to the west-southwest and Little Matterhorn to the northwest. Enjoy it all before retracing your route back to Bear Lake.

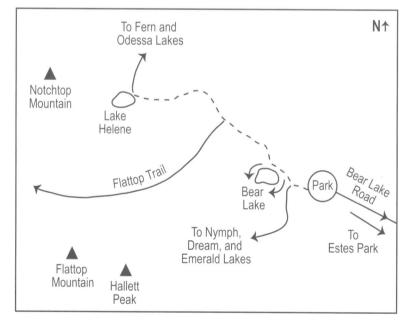

Lake Helene and Notchtop Mountain

Hike Distance: 2.9 miles each way

Hiking Time: Out in 88 minutes. Back in 82 minutes.

Starting Elevation: 9,400 feet

Highest Elevation: 10,680 feet

Elevation Gain: 1,454 feet (includes 174 extra feet)

Trail: All the way

Relevant Maps: Trails Illustrated 200 or 301

   McHenrys Peak 7½ minute

   Larimer County Number Three

   Rocky Mountain National Park (available at entrance)

   Roosevelt National Forest

84 Surprise Lake

This hike to Surprise Lake in the Eagles Nest Wilderness takes you through aspen groves and lush meadows, which are sometimes used to graze cattle. The trail intersects the Gore Range Trail and continues past Surprise Lake to other lakes. A loop hike is also possible passing Tipperary Lake and returning to Lower Cataract Lake and the Surprise Lake Trailhead.

Getting There: From I-70 at Dillon and Silverthorne, take Exit 205 and drive north on CO 9 for 16.7 miles and take the left fork, just before Green Mountain Reservoir, onto Road 30, which leads to Heeney and beyond. Continue on Road 30 for 5.6 miles and turn sharply left onto unpaved Road 1725. Drive up this road for 2.3 miles and park at the Surprise Trailhead. On this final segment on the dirt road, keep left at mile 1.3, right at mile 2.1, and left at mile 2.2. Regular cars can readily reach this trailhead.

The Hike: Begin to the south and cross Cataract Creek on a bridge. Then ascend the trail steeply into the forest and pass through several meadows as you proceed upward to a sign and a junction with the Gore Range Trail at mile 2.9. Continue to the right another 0.1 mile and beautiful Surprise Lake will appear on the left. Water lilies abound in the lake, and Dora Mountain is impressive to the south-southeast. The trail continues, but if this is your destination, return as you came.

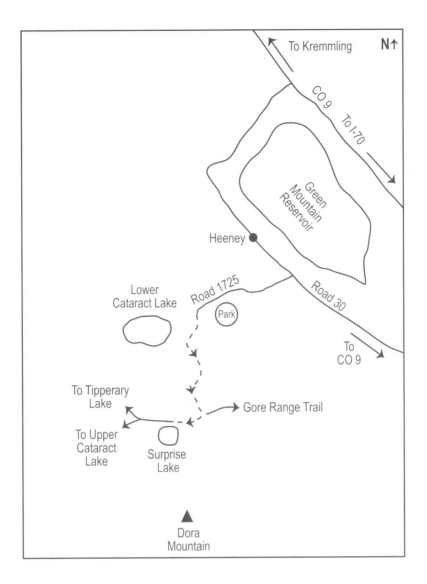

Hike Distance: 3.0 miles each way

Hiking Time: Up in 95 minutes. Down in 69 minutes.

Starting Elevation: 8,580 feet

Highest Elevation: 10,044 feet

Elevation Gain: 1,688 feet (includes 112 extra feet each way)

Trail: All the way

Relevant Maps: Trails Illustrated 107 or 149

    Mount Powell 7½ minute

    Summit County Number One

    Arapaho National Forest—Dillon Ranger District

85 Bridal Veil Falls

This hike to Bridal Veil Falls utilizes the excellent trail system of Rocky Mountain National Park, yet no park fee is required. Pets and vehicles are forbidden. The trail is gradual and steepens just before you reach the lovely waterfall. Spring is an ideal time for this outing with the snow melt from Mummy Mountain feeding the falls. Some slight snow cover may still be encountered until early May.

Getting There: From the junction of U.S. 34 and U.S. 36 in Estes Park drive west on U.S. 34 for 0.4 mile and turn right onto MacGregor Avenue, which becomes Devils Gulch Road. McGraw Ranch Road will be 3.8 miles from the U.S. 36 and U.S. 34 intersection in Estes Park. Drive on the good dirt road toward McGraw Ranch and set your mileage to zero. Keep straight at 1 mile, left at 1.1 miles, and park at 2.1 miles off the road, just before crossing a bridge to the former McGraw Ranch.

Hike Distance: 3.2 miles each way

Hiking Time: Up in 76 minutes. Down in 68 minutes.

Starting Elevation: 7,830 feet

Highest Elevation: 8,720 feet

Elevation Gain: 1,380 feet (includes 245 extra feet each way)

Trail: All the way

Relevant Maps: Trails Illustrated 200

Estes Park 7½ minute

Larimer County Number Four

Roosevelt National Forest

Rocky Mountain National Park

The Hike: Cross the bridge over Cow Creek on foot and pass to the right of the Cow Creek Trailhead signboard on the clear trail through the former McGraw Ranch. Follow the trail as it turns left and runs parallel to Cow Creek on the left. After a few hundred yards from the trailhead, keep left at a fork and stay on the Cow Creek Trail. After 1.2 miles from the trailhead, go straight at a signed fork and continue southwest up the valley. (The left fork goes to Gem Lake.) Pass Rabbit Ears Campsite on your left and within a mile, take the right fork at a sign. You will make two creek crossings and in 0.8 mile from the last fork you will reach a corral. Ascend the trail more steeply and always keep Cow Creek on your left, as the trail crosses some flat rock. In several hundred yards from the corral, the trail ends at the foot of photogenic Bridal Veil Falls. Enjoy the falls and the mist before retracing your route back.

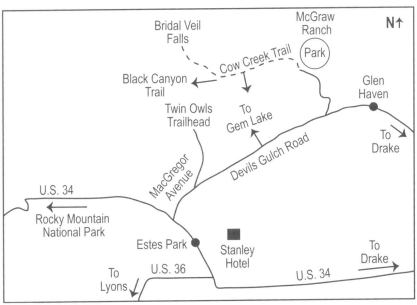

86 Gold Creek Lake

Hike Distance: 3.1 miles each way

Hiking Time: Up in 80 minutes. Down in 68 minutes.

Starting Elevation: 8,440 feet

Highest Elevation: 9,572 feet

Elevation Gain: 1,612 feet (includes 240 extra feet each way)

Trail: All the way

Relevant Maps: Trails Illustrated 116

Mount Zirkel 7½ minute

Routt County Number Two

Routt National Forest

Taree Muller at Gold Creek Lake

ocated at the edge of the Routt Divide Blowdown of October 1997, the popular trail to Gold Creek Lake is especially beautiful. The rushing waters of Gold Creek parallel the trail and provide waterfalls, cascades, and a few creek crossings. Since one creek can be difficult to cross, try this hike after mid-August when the runoff is diminished.

Getting There: From U.S. 40 west of Steamboat Springs, drive northwest on Routt County Road 129 for 17.6 miles. Then turn right onto Seedhouse Road (Forest Road 400) just after passing through the town of Clark. Follow Seedhouse Road for 11.8 miles to the end of the road at the Slavonia Trailhead. En route, take the right fork at mile 8.6, go straight at mile 9.2 and left at mile 9.4. Regular cars can drive this good dirt road to the trailhead.

The Hike: Follow the trail from signs at the end of the parking area and enter lush forest to the north-northeast. Within 75 yards, the trail forks at a register and sign. Proceed east on the right fork. The clear trail is overgrown in places, but there are many clearings and overlook areas along the way. Soon cross over a bridge and continue up the valley. Two miles from the trailhead, there is a creek crossing on a large log, followed closely by an easier crossing over rocks. The final mile to the lake uses several switchbacks and passes through an area of fallen trees just before reaching beautiful Gold Creek Lake with the ridge of Flattop Mountain visible to the northeast. The trail continues another mile to a fork with Gilpin Lake to the left and Mount Zirkel and the Continental Divide to the right. Return by your ascent trail unless you want a longer loop, then return via Gilpin Lake back to the Slavonia Trailhead.

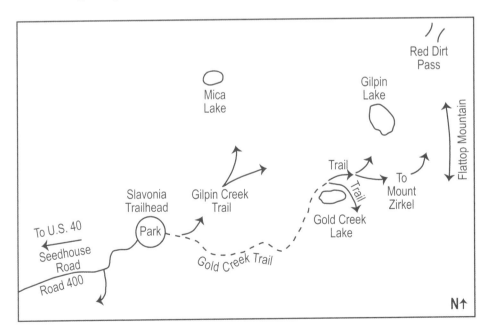

Hike Distance: 2.4 miles each way

Hiking Time: Up in 75 minutes. Down in 65 minutes.

Starting Elevation: 10,875 feet

Highest Elevation: 11,902 feet

Elevation Gain: 1,071 feet
(includes 22 extra feet each way)

Trail: Initial 0.8 mile

Relevant Maps: Trails Illustrated 105

Topaz Mountain 7½ minute

Park County Number Two

Pike National Forest

Views From the Summit: N to North Twin Cone Peak

SSE to Tarryall Reservoir

SE to Bison Peak, McCurdy Mountain, Pikes Peak, and Topaz Mountain

WSW to Horseshoe Mountain

North Tarryall Peak from Topaz Mountain

A great overlook of South Park awaits you at the top of North Tarryall Peak. Bring your compass or GPS since the upper part of the route has no trail. The season for this hike is from the second half of June through October.

Getting There: From Kenosha Pass southwest of Bailey, drive on U.S. 285 to the southwest for 2.9 miles. Near Jefferson, turn left onto Lost Park Road (Park County 56) and continue 13.5 more miles on the good dirt road. Here turn right onto Road 446 (Topaz Road) and drive 2.4 miles and park on the left in a large open area. Most regular cars can reach this point.

The Hike: Start from the road to the west-southwest on the Nate Stultz Trail, which quickly enters the woods and crosses Monkey Creek. Follow the occasionally faint trail 0.8 mile to a junction with an old logging road. Go left here and within 150 yards, make another crossing of modest Monkey Creek. A good route from here is to leave the road and ascend to the right (northwest). Keep the creek, and eventually the extensive willows, always on your right. At the upper segment of the drainage, veer left (west) and ascend through a forested and burn area to the right side of prominent North Tarryall Peak. The final 50 yards, over tundra and rocks, brings you to a wooden tower, a cairn, and a benchmark at the summit. Enjoy the vistas. The return retraces your ascent.

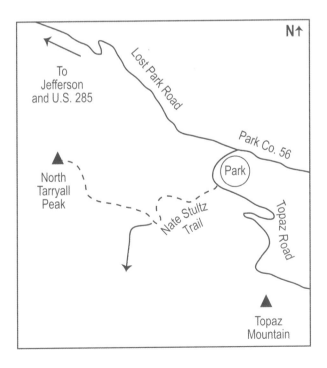

88 Deer Mountain

Mount Ypsilon from Deer Mountain

Hike Distance: 3.1 miles each way

Hiking Time: Up in 100 minutes. Down in 80 minutes.

Starting Elevation: 8,930 feet

Highest Elevation: 10,013 feet

Elevation Gain: 1,723 feet (includes 320 extra feet each way)

Trail: All the way

Relevant Maps: Trails Illustrated 200 or 301

    Estes Park 7½ minute

    Rocky Mountain National Park

    Larimer County Number Three

    Roosevelt National Forest

Views From the Summit: NNW to Mummy Mountain

    NW to Mount Ypsilon

    ENE to Lake Estes

    S to Longs Peak

    SSE to Lily Mountain and Estes Cone

    SSW to Hallett Peak and Flattop Mountain

    SE to Twin Sisters Peaks

D eer Mountain is a popular hiking destination on the eastern side of beautiful Rocky Mountain National Park. The good trail rises steeply to a saddle before descending 0.5 mile and then climbing steeply to the flat summit with a great panorama of Longs Peak and adjacent mountains. As with all trails in the park, pets, bicycles, and weapons are forbidden. No flowing water will be encountered.

Getting There: From the Beaver Meadows Entrance to Rocky Mountain National Park, west of Estes Park, drive west 0.2 mile. Keep straight at the intersection and avoid Bear Lake Road on the left. Continue another 2.8 miles and park on the right at the Deer Mountain Trailhead.

The Hike: Begin north at the trailhead sign. After 0.1 mile through the thin forest, keep right and ascending as a trail descends left to the Aspenglen Campground. Ascend the open southern flank of Deer Mountain with gorgeous views of Longs Peak across the valley. After several switchbacks, arrive at a flat, tree-covered saddle and then continue by trail about 0.5 mile to a sign at a fork. Take the upward trail on the right and follow it steeply to a large cairn and a nearby benchmark at the flat summit. Take some pictures and enjoy your vantage point before returning as you came.

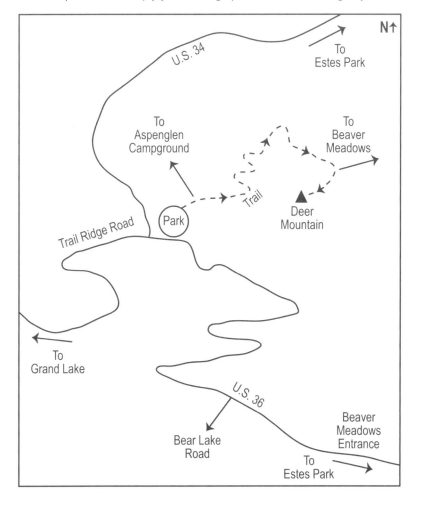

89

Inter-Laken and Dexter's Cabin

Hike Distance: 3.5 miles each way

Hiking Time: Out in 85 minutes. Back in 91 minutes.

Starting Elevation: 9,320 feet

Highest Elevation: 9,390 feet

Elevation Gain: 944 feet (includes 874 extra feet)

Trail: All the way

Relevant Maps: Trails Illustrated 110 and 127 or 148

Granite 7½ minute

Mount Elbert 7½ minute

Lake County

San Isabel National Forest

Colorado Trail Number Ten

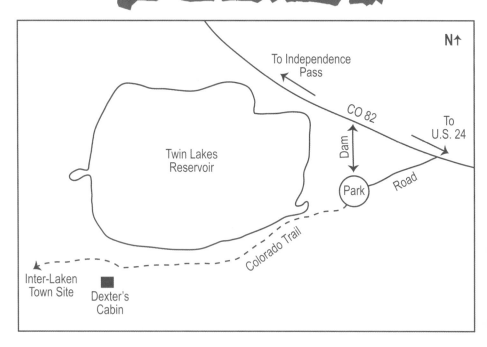

nter-Laken and Dexter's Cabin, remnants of Colorado history, can be reached from either the east or west by the Colorado Trail. The western approach from the Willis Gulch Trailhead, just off of CO 82, west of the town of Twin Lakes, will be described here. There are several specific features of this hike. Two large, beautiful lakes lie to the north of the trail and are visible during the final third of your outward route. Many of Colorado's highest peaks can be seen from the trail, the aspen gold is abundant in mid- to late-September, and the history of Inter-Laken and Dexter's Cabin is well-told by several signs at their location. Inter-Laken was a popular resort in the late 1800s. James V. Dexter owned the resort and built a home for himself nearby. Dexter was involved in mining and banking and died in 1899.

Getting There: From U.S. 24 between Leadville and Buena Vista, drive west on CO 82 for 8.5 miles and turn left onto a dirt road at a Willis Gulch Trailhead sign. Follow this road 0.1 mile until it ends near the trailhead signboard and Lake Creek.

The Hike: Begin to the south, cross a bridge over Lake Creek and continue straight (south) and avoid side trails on the left and right. Within 100 yards from the trailhead, go left (southeast) at a signed fork. Always stay on the good main trail as it rises over a ridge, which is the highest point on this hike. Avoid a right fork to Willis Gulch. Cross a few small creeks and reach a four-way intersection at mile 1.3 of your hike. Continue straight (east-northeast) on the Colorado Trail, which also ascends to the right. Cross Boswell Gulch and a meadow before arriving at 8 preserved structures and informative signs at the Inter-Laken and Dexter's Cabin sites. As you reflect on the history of this location, enjoy this scenic setting near the edge of the Lower Twin Lake. Retrace your route back to the Willis Gulch Trailhead, unless you have a second vehicle at the eastern edge of the Twin Lakes, or you want a longer hike.

Dexter's Cabin

90

Bald Eagle Mountain

View to the southwest from Bald Eagle Mountain

B ald Eagle Mountain lies west of a segment of the Colorado Trail (formerly the Main Range Trail) and provides good views of Mount Elbert and Mount Massive, the two highest peaks in Colorado.

Getting There: From U.S. 24 (Harrison Avenue) in central Leadville, drive west on West Sixth Street for 0.8 mile and turn right at the T. Keep left after 0.1 mile and go straight in 0.9 mile. After 1.6 miles farther, take the right fork and stay on the paved road. Keep straight for 0.9 mile and again 1.4 miles farther. In 2.0 more miles, take the left fork and leave the paved road (which will continue around Turquoise Lake). After driving 0.9 miles on this good dirt road, park on the side of the road when two sign poles indicate the Colorado Trail.

The Hike: From the south side of the road, begin southeast on the Colorado Trail and ascend in 1.2 miles to a dirt road running east and west. Leave the trail at this point and bushwhack up to the southwest. Pass under some power lines and in 1.0 mile from the Colorado Trail, pass over the tundra to reach the flat summit area just above tree line. The high point lies on the southwest edge of the summit mesa and consists of several vertical boulders. A wooden tripod and a nearby USGS marker can be found at a lower point on the northeast part of the mesa.

Hike Distance: 2.2 miles each way

Hiking Time: Up in 76 minutes. Down in 60 minutes.

Starting Elevation: 10,360 feet

Highest Elevation: 11,913 feet

Elevation Gain: 1,573 feet (includes 10 extra feet each way)

Trail: Initial 1.2 miles

Relevant Maps: Trails Illustrated 126 or 149

    Homestake Reservoir 7½ minute

    Lake County

    San Isabel National Forest

    Colorado Trail Map Number Nine

Views From the Summit: N to Homestake Peak

    NNE to Jaque Peak

    NNW to Mount of the Holy Cross and Galena Mountain

    NE to Sugarloaf Mountain, Buckeye Peak, and Turquoise Lake

    ENE to Mount Sherman

    SSE to Mount Harvard and Mount Elbert

    SSW to Mount Massive

    SE to East Buffalo Peak and West Buffalo Peak

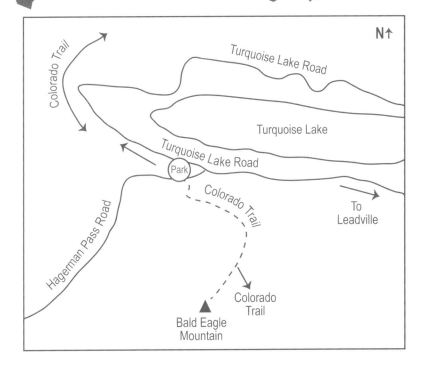

91 Carpenter Peak

With its beautiful red rock formations and fine network of trails, Roxborough State Park is a special place. Of the many trails, the most demanding rises to the top of Carpenter Peak. Dogs are forbidden in the park, and horses and bicycles are not allowed on this trail. Be sure to read the informational signs about mountain lions and rattlesnakes!

Getting There: Drive south on U.S. 85 from its juncture with C-470 for 4.4 miles and turn right (west) on Titan Road. Follow Titan Road, which becomes Douglas County Road 7, and then Road 5 for 7 miles as it curves left (southwest). Turn left on Douglas County Road 3, go for 100 yards and take the road on the right; 2.2 miles on this road brings you to the parking area for Roxborough State Park. An entry fee is charged.

The Hike: Begin to the south-southwest across from the visitor center. Enter the oak trees and keep right at two well-marked forks. After 0.5 mile from the trailhead, cross a dirt road and continue straight at a sign. Soon take a right fork as a trail to the left rises to an overlook. You now ascend clockwise to a treeless area on a ridge, which affords the first viewing of Carpenter Peak. You have traveled 1.75 miles so far. On the way to this overlook, the views of the gorgeous red rock formations have been frequent and you pass two of three memorial benches that line this trail. Continue down north-northwest from the ridge and then up through the sparse forest to a signed fork near the summit. The left trail leads to Waterton Canyon in 3 miles and to the Colorado Trail in 4.4 miles. Follow the right trail to the unmarked rocky summit and good viewing within 100 yards. Enjoy your high perch before returning as you ascended back to the visitor center.

Hike Distance: 3.2 miles each way

Hiking Time: Up in 92 minutes. Down in 78 minutes.

Starting Elevation: 6,200 feet

Highest Elevation: 7,205 feet

Elevation Gain: 1,645 feet (includes 640 extra feet)

Trail: All the way

Relevant Maps: Trails Illustrated 135

  Roxborough State Park

  Kassler 7½ minute

  Douglas County Number One

  Pike National Forest

Views From the Summit: N to Denver

  NNW to Chatfield Reservoir

  SE to Pikes Peak

  SW to Long Scraggy Peak and Windy Peak

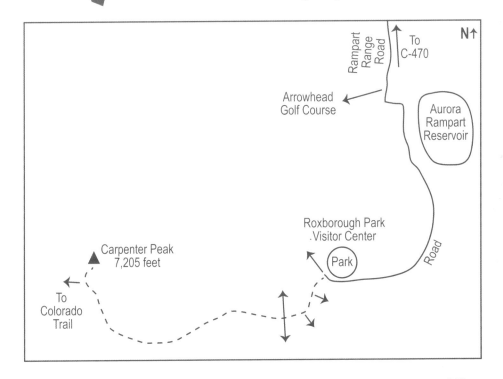

92

Silver Dollar Lake and Murray Lake

Here is a beautiful hike in a popular area. The trail quickly passes timberline south of Naylor Lake (on private property), continues west to Silver Dollar Lake, and rises over tundra to isolated Murray Lake, with Mount Wilcox looming above to the north, Argentine Peak to the west, and Square Top Mountain to the southsoutheast.

Getting There: From the four-way intersection at Sixth and Rose Streets, with stop signs in the center of Georgetown, drive south on Guanella Pass Road for 8.9 miles and turn right. The Guanella Pass Road is designated Road 381 north of the pass and Road 62 south of the pass. Drive up the steep dirt road for 0.6 mile and park in the designated area on the right. Most regular cars with good clearance can reach this point.

The Hike: Begin south-southwest from the trail sign, and in 0.8 mile reach timberline. The vistas from here onward are lovely. Naylor Lake lies below to the north. Continue west and in 1.6 miles from the trailhead reach lovely, round, Silver Dollar Lake on the left. Continue southwest up the trail, which then curves north and leads you directly 0.4 mile to secluded Murray Lake, which drains into Naylor Lake. The Continental Divide is an easy mile to the west if you wish to explore farther.

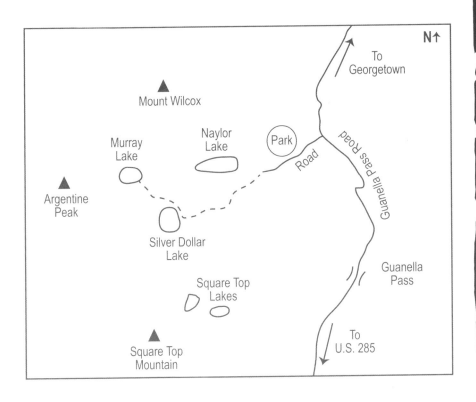

Hike Distance: 2.0 miles each way

Hiking Time: Up in 66 minutes. Down in 48 minutes.

Starting Elevation: 11,160 feet

Highest Elevation: 12,336 feet

Elevation Gain: 1,581 feet (includes 405 extra feet)

Trail: All the way except the last 100 yards

Relevant Maps: Trails Illustrated 104

    Mount Evans 7½ minute

    Montezuma 7½ minute

    Clear Creek County

    Arapaho National Forest

93 | Mill Lake

The relatively short upward trek to Mill Lake in the Fossil Ridge Wilderness rewards the hiker with a serene, green lake beneath Fossil Mountain. Bicycles and all motorized vehicles are forbidden in the wilderness areas.

Getting There: On U.S. 50 east of Gunnison, drive to Parlin and turn north on Gunnison Road 76, which leads to Ohio City. After 7.5 miles on this road, turn left at Ohio City onto Road 771 and follow it for 6.7 miles near the Gold Creek Campground and park on the left near the trailhead sign. Regular cars can readily reach this point.

The Hike: From the sign at the trailhead, walk up to the north-northwest, through an open meadow and into the trees. After 0.4 mile, take the right fork to Mill Lake at signs and a trail register. The left fork takes you on the Fossil Ridge Trail to Boulder Lake and beyond. By ascending the trail on the right, you enter the Fossil Ridge Wilderness. It is a little over 2 miles from here to Mill Lake. En route, you cross two creeks and pass through a clearing full of fallen timber about 1 mile below the lake. Follow the good trail with its many switchbacks until it ends at the lake in a grassy bowl. Fossil Mountain lies above to the west. Return as you ascended.

Hike Distance: 2.5 miles each way

Hiking Time: Up in 75 minutes. Down in 50 minutes.

Starting Elevation: 10,030 feet

Highest Elevation: 11,470 feet

Elevation Gain: 1,540 feet (includes 50 extra feet each way)

Trail: All the way

Relevant Maps: Trails Illustrated 132

    Fairview Peak 7½ minute

    Gunnison County Number Five

    Gunnison Basin Area

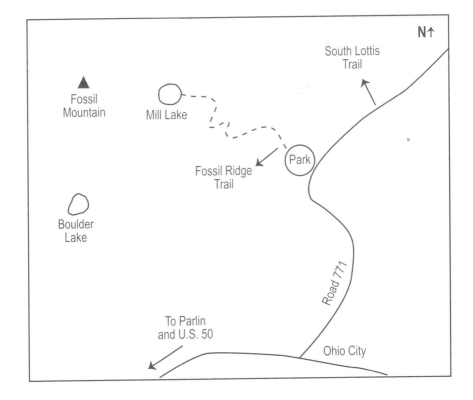

Mitchell Lake and Blue Lake

Mitchell Lake and Mount Toll in the center background

Hike Distance: 2.8 miles each way

Hiking Time: Up in 66 minutes. Down in 60 minutes.

Starting Elevation: 10,460 feet

Highest Elevation: 11,300 feet

Elevation Gain: 1,000 feet (includes 80 extra feet each way)

Trail: All the way

Relevant Maps: Trails Illustrated 102

   Ward 7½ minute

   Boulder County

   Roosevelt National Forest

O f the many lakes called Blue Lake in Colorado, this one in the Indian Peaks Wilderness is my nominee for most scenic. After passing lovely Mitchell Lake, the trail crosses much flowing water before arriving at Blue Lake, which lies at tree line in a bowl encircled by four of the Indian Peaks: Pawnee Peak, Mount Toll, Paiute Peak, and Mount Audubon. This is a very popular hiking area and excellent for families.

Getting There: Drive northwest from Nederland on CO 72 for 11.7 miles and turn left onto Brainard Lake Road. Continue for 5.7 miles on this paved road to the Mitchell Lake Trailhead. En route, keep right at mile 5.2 and at mile 5.3. Park in the large designated area.

The Hike: Start to the southwest from the Mitchell Lake Trailhead. Cross a bridge after 0.4 mile and pass a wilderness sign. After 1 mile from the trailhead, Mitchell Lake will appear on your right. Take some time to explore this lake and the vistas to the west. Resume toward Blue Lake and soon cross a creek on logs, pass some small unnamed ponds, finally ascend to timberline on the excellent trail and reach scenic Blue Lake. Pawnee Peak looms above to the south-southwest (left), Mount Toll to the west-southwest, Paiute Peak to the west-northwest, and Mount Audubon to the northwest (right).

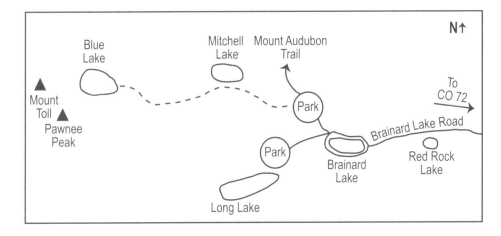

95 Sleepy Lion—Button Rock Trails

V ast green meadows grace this outing near the Ralph Price Reservoir. At the highest and farthest point, the trail connects with trails of the Hall Valley Ranch Park. Bicycles are forbidden on both trails, and no dogs are allowed on the Button Rock Trail.

Getting There: From the intersection with CO 7 at the western edge of Lyons, drive northwest on U.S. 36 for 4 miles. Then turn left on County Road 80 and drive on this main road 2.7 miles and park at the end of the road at a trailhead barrier.

The Hike: Begin west from the road barrier and ascend a wide road past the Longmont Reservoir on the right. After 0.6 mile take the Sleepy Lion Trail on the left. This trail rises to a large meadow. At mile 1.9 go left at signs and a fork. You are now in Hall Ranch Park, which is part of the North Foothills Open Space. Descend a short distance and take a left fork, which leads to a large open field and past a large rock formation before reaching the Nighthawk Trail. This is the turnaround point.

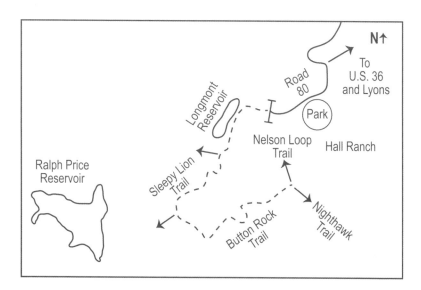

Hike Distance: 3.5 miles each way

Hiking Time: Up in 98 minutes. Down in 92 minutes.

Starting Elevation: 5,940 feet

Highest Elevation: 6,700 feet

Elevation Gain: 1,110 feet (includes 175 extra feet each way)

Trail: All the way

Relevant Maps: Trails Illustrated 100

    Lyons 7½ minute

    Hall Valley Ranch Park

    Button Rock Preserve

    Boulder County

    Roosevelt National Forest

Group near high point of Button Rock Trail

96

New York Mountain

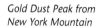

*Gold Dust Peak from
New York Mountain*

Hike Distance: 2.4 miles each way

Hiking Time: Up in 70 minutes.
Down in 50 minutes.

Starting Elevation: 11,360 feet

Highest Elevation: 12,550 feet

Elevation Gain: 1,320 feet
(includes 65 extra feet each way)

Trail: Initial 1.9 miles

Relevant Maps: Trails Illustrated 121 or 149

Fulford 7½ minute

Grouse Mountain 7½ minute

Eagle County Numbers Three and Four

White River National Forest

Views From the Summit: NNE to Polar Star Lake

ESE to Mount Jackson

SSW to Nolan Lake

SE to Gold Dust Peak

SW to Capitol Peak, Craig Mountain, and
Mount Sopris

The most difficult part of this hike is getting to the trailhead. The many intersections on the long dirt road are complicated. Use the maps and my directions. New York Mountain is a long series of summits in the Holy Cross Wilderness. Several other inviting peaks and lakes are located in this remote area.

Getting There: Take Exit 147 from I-70 and drive south to the old town of Eagle. After 0.4 mile take the first left turn onto Capitol Street and set your mileage to zero. Continue south on Capitol Street and at 0.7 mile turn left onto Brush Creek Road, which is also designated Eagle County Road 307. Follow Brush Creek Road up the valley and turn left at mile 10.3 just before a creek crossing. Follow the good dirt road and continue straight at mile 14.5 and again at mile 16.2. (The Yeoman Park Campground will be on the right.) Take the left fork at mile 16.5, pass a road to Fulford on the left. Continue straight on Road 418 at mile 19.8. Keep right at mile 22.1. Take the left fork at mile 24.0 and again at mile 25.1. At mile 25.7 park on the left at the New York Mountain Trailhead. You are still on Road 418. (The road is blocked a few hundred yards farther.) Regular cars with good clearance can reach this trailhead.

The Hike: Begin to the east from the trailhead sign. Pass a wilderness sign and curve to the right through the trees. The trail then leads through the remnants of the Polar Star Mine and then crosses an old mining road. (Ascend left on it to gain the New York Lake Trail.) Continue straight (east) across this road and soon traverse a series of talus and tundra slopes. An old pipeline parallels the trail. Eventually the trail passes the old Johnson Mine and curves up through tundra to the east to reach a ridge on the shoulder of New York Mountain. At the ridge, continue gradually up and northeast with no trail to the highest of the summits on the peak. Some cairns may help to direct you. At the high point, there is a large rock pile. Explore the nearby remote terrain before returning as you ascended.

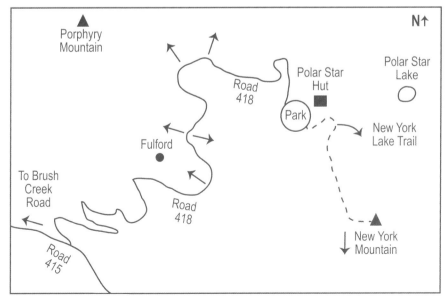

97

Greenhorn Mountain

Greenhorn Mountain at right

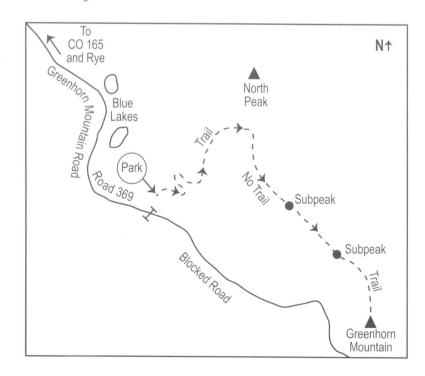

Greenhorn Mountain lies on the border between Pueblo and Huerfano Counties. It is the highest peak in Pueblo County and is named after a Comanche tribal leader. Of the various routes to the top, this one involves more driving and less hiking. The forest roads, which bring you to the trailhead past many side roads and trails, are pleasant and picturesque.

Getting There: From Exit 74 off I-25 south of Pueblo, drive west on CO 165 through Colorado City and Rye for a total of 25.1 miles from I-25. Then turn left onto Road 360 at the sign for the Ophir Creek Campground. Follow wide and well-graded Road 360 for 1.2 miles and go left at an intersection. At mile 8.1 from CO 165, go left at a four-way intersection onto Road 369. Follow this good road another 16.2 miles to the end of the road and park on the left at the trailhead sign. En route to this parking area, stay on the main road and pass the two Blue Lakes on the left 0.4 mile before you park. The road becomes a bit rougher after the Blue Lakes, but regular cars can reach the trailhead.

The Hike: From the trailhead where the Greenhorn Mountain Road is blocked, begin east at the trail sign. Pass a Greenhorn Mountain Wilderness sign and enter the trees as the trail turns right and then switchbacks up to a shelf trail leading directly to a saddle with North Peak on the left and grassy subpeaks on the right. Greenhorn Mountain will not be visible until you cross the westerly subpeak. From the saddle, leave the trail and ascend the ridge on grassy, gentle slopes to the south (right). Cross over the hill at 12,000 feet and descend 150 feet to another saddle. Keep to the left of the next subpeak and aim toward the highest trees on the left side of the ridge. Several faint trails may be evident. Continue east-southeast up the ridge past trees on your left on a more definite trail. Proceed past some rock shelters to another rock shelter and a register at the Greenhorn Mountain summit. The views can be great from here. Enjoy and return as you ascended. North Peak is an easy side trip on the way back.

Hike Distance: 3.3 miles each way

Hiking Time: Up in 80 minutes. Down in 70 minutes.

Starting Elevation: 11,470 feet

Highest Elevation: 12,347 feet

Elevation Gain: 1,377 feet (includes 250 extra feet each way)

Trail: Initial 1.2 miles and final 1.4 miles

Relevant Maps: San Isabel 7½ minute
Huerfano County Number Two
Pueblo County Number Three
San Isabel National Forest

Views From the Summit: NNW to Pikes Peak
NE to Colorado City
SSE to East and West Spanish Peaks
SW to Mount Blanca
WNW to Crestone Needle, Crestone Peak, Kit Carson Peak, and Humboldt Peak

98 Mosca Pass

Hike Distance: 3.3 miles each way

Hiking Time: Up in 94 minutes. Down in 74 minutes.

Starting Elevation: 8,225 feet

Highest Elevation: 9,730 feet

Elevation Gain: 1,685 feet (includes 90 extra feet each way)

Trail: All the way

Relevant Maps: Trails Illustrated 138 or 149

Mosca Pass 7½ minute

Zapata Ranch 7½ minute

Rio Grande National Forest

Alamosa County

Wilderness Boundary near Mosca Pass

One of the best Great Sand Dune hikes leads to Mosca Pass. Mosca means "fly" in Spanish. Bicycles are forbidden and dogs must be leashed. The route rises through aspen trees to the pass 100 yards east of the wilderness boundary. The views from the pass are not special, but if you take the dead-end road southeast from just beyond the pass, there is a great overlook to the east and southeast within 300 yards. Mount Lindsey can be seen to the south-southeast and the Spanish Peaks to the east and east-southeast.

Getting There: From the visitor center in the Great Sand Dunes National Park, drive north 0.2 mile to the Montville Nature Center and Mosca Pass Trailhead on the right and park.

The Hike: Begin to the east past trail signs and a register on the Montville Nature Trail. Quickly reach a fork and keep to the right. Pass a plaque on a boulder before crossing a bridge at an intersection. The left fork is part of the nature trail. Continue up to the right through lush forest. Occasional rock formations and cacti are present alongside the trail before you pass through two small meadows before reaching the Sangre de Cristo Wilderness boundary. A few more minutes on foot brings you to Mosca Pass at an intersection with a benchmark on the left at the side of the road. Check out the overlook to the southeast before returning to your starting point.

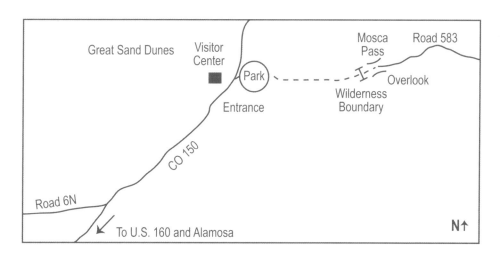

99 Mount Argentine

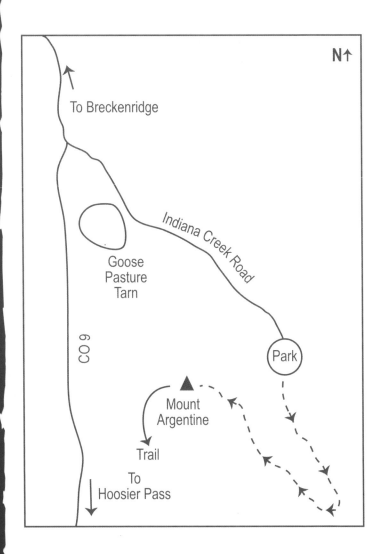

Hike Distance: 2.7 miles each way

Hiking Time: Up in 88 minutes. Down in 72 minutes.

Starting Elevation: 10,350 feet

Highest Elevation: 11,412 feet

Elevation Gain: 1,432 feet (includes 185 extra feet each way)

Trail: All the way

Relevant Maps: Trails Illustrated 109 or 149

Breckenridge 7½ minute

Summit County Number Two

Arapaho National Forest—Dillon Ranger District

Views From the Summit: N to Ptarmigan Peak

NNW to Buffalo Mountain

NW to Peak 8, Breckenridge, Peak 2, and Peak 1

E to Bald Mountain

ESE to Boreas Mountain

SSE to Red Mountain

SSW to Mount Bross

SW to Mount Lincoln, North Star Mountain, and Quandary Peak

WSW to Pacific Peak, Mount Helen, and Crystal Peak

This easy hike to obscure Mount Argentine offers a beautiful summit mountain panorama. Located south of Breckenridge above Indiana Creek, this 11,000-foot mountain should not be confused with Argentine Peak, which is higher and lies west of the Guanella Pass Road above Georgetown.

Getting There: From South Park Avenue in Breckenridge, drive south on CO 9 for 1.3 miles and turn left onto Indiana Creek Road. Set your mileage to zero. Keep left at 0.3 mile and again at 0.7 mile. Continue on the public access road through a private ranch. The road becomes unpaved and rough. Park off the side of the road at mile 2.5. Regular cars can come this far. Four-wheel drive can take you farther up Indiana Creek Road.

The Hike: Begin on foot up the rough road to the south-southeast. Stay on the main road and keep right at every junction that you encounter. After crossing Indiana Creek, the ascent steepens somewhat and arrives at a T and saddle. Continue to the right (north-northwest) and quickly reach a trail on the right as the road curves left and descends. Take this trail to the north-northwest as it meanders up and down along a ridge before reaching a flat, semi-open summit with great views. A rock pile near the high point is the only marker. The trail continues down to the southwest from the last fork, but the return is by your ascent route.

207

Hike Distance: 2.4 miles each way

Hiking Time: Up in 70 minutes. Down in 54 minutes.

Starting Elevation: 10,360 feet

Highest Elevation: 11,969 feet

Elevation Gain: 1,650 feet (includes 41 extra feet)

Trail: All the way

Relevant Maps: Trails Illustrated 109 or 149

Breckenridge 7½ minute

Summit County Number Two

Arapaho National Forest (Dillon Ranger District)

Lower Crystal Lake and Father Dyer Peak

M any people don't realize that high country hiking remains possible in Colorado well into November. It is colder and the wind is often strong, but the late fall colors and scenery can be rewarding. Spruce Creek Road, south of Breckenridge, offers many hiking and cross-country ski routes. (Four-wheel-drive vehicles can ascend past the 1.3-mile mark from CO 9 and reach several high points including Lower Crystal Lake and the Mohawk Lakes Trailhead.)

Getting There: Drive south on CO 9 from Ski Hill Road in the center of Breckenridge for 2.7 miles. Then turn right and drive up Spruce Creek Road for a total of 1.3 miles and park near a trail sign. En route to this point, stay on the main road and take left forks at mile 0.15 and 0.2 and keep straight at mile 0.5, 0.6, and 0.7. Regular cars can reach this parking area at mile 1.3.

The Hike: Begin up Spruce Creek Road and after 0.2 mile take the right (west) fork toward Lower Crystal Lake. This is an old mining road and quite steep. Keep straight, as a trail intersects the road 0.15 mile above the fork. Ascend the road generally west through the trees for 1.7 miles from your vehicle and pass an intersection of the Wheeler Trail, which runs north and south. Continue up the old mining road, cross Crystal Creek, and ascend to a bench and a cabin ruin at a fork in the road. Take the right fork and reach Lower Crystal Lake within 150 yards. Impressive peaks rise around the lake. Mount Helen lies to the south-southeast, Crystal Peak to the west-southwest, and Peak 10 to the northwest. The high peak to the southwest of the lake is Father Dyer Peak. Bald Mountain can be seen looking back to the east-northeast. This is the destination of this hike, but the road continues up to the west and northwest to enable ready access to Crystal Peak, Peak 10, and Upper Crystal Lake.

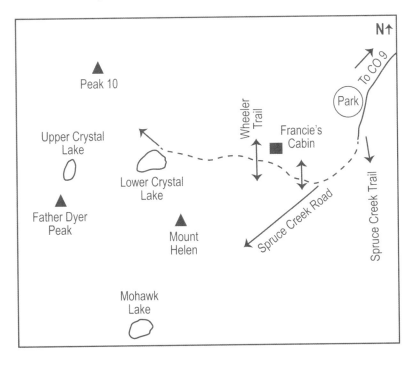

101 Butler Gulch to Tree Line

The vast basin above tree line at the head of Butler Gulch is worth the effort. There is little summer traffic in Butler Gulch, but lots of Nordic ski and snow-shoe activity in the winter.

Getting There: From U.S. 40 between Empire and Berthoud Pass, drive west at the big right curve of U.S. 40 (from the east). Pass the Big Bend Picnic Ground, avoid a road on the left 0.4 mile from U.S. 40, and after another 1.1 miles, ascend Jones Pass Road just before the Henderson Mine. Follow this road up 0.8 mile to a fork and park near a road barrier on the left.

The Hike: Start out down from the barrier on the wide road that winds up steep Butler Gulch. Cross two modest creeks, and finally emerge from the trees and enter a vast basin surrounded by high peaks. The road is narrow at times as it curves upward to reach a high point and a pole in a rock pile. Vasquez Peak is visible north-northeast and Red Mountain to the east.

Hike Distance: 2.4 miles each way

Hiking Time: Up in 78 minutes. Down in 70 minutes.

Starting Elevation: 10,434 feet

Highest Elevation: 11,910 feet

Elevation Gain: 1,614 feet (includes 69 extra feet each way)

Trail: All the way

Relevant Maps: Trails Illustrated 103

    Berthoud Pass 7½ minute

    Clear Creek County

    Arapaho National Forest

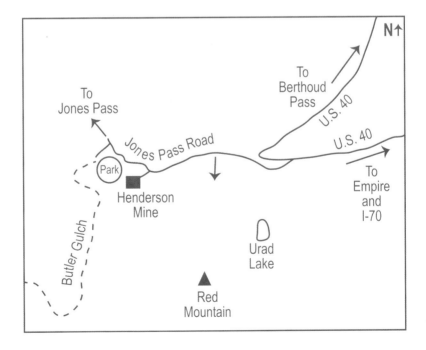

102 Kite Lake and Lake Emma

Hike Distance: 1.4 miles to Kite Lake, 1.0 mile farther to Lake Emma

Hiking Time: 35 minutes up to Kite Lake, 30 more minutes to Lake Emma. Down in 45 minutes.

Starting Elevation: 11,350 feet

Highest Elevation: 12,630 feet

Elevation Gain: 1,350 feet (includes 35 extra feet each way)

Trail: All the way

Relevant Maps: Trails Illustrated 109

Climax 7½ minute

Alma 7½ minute

Park County Number One

Pike National Forest

This hike starts at an abandoned mine and ascends an old mining road to Kite Lake, which is bordered on three sides by fourteeners. Then leave the majority of hikers climbing Mount Democrat and ascend southwest to rugged Lake Emma at the foot of Mount Democrat.

Getting There: From the town of Alma on CO 9, drive west on a dirt road opposite the post office and a gas station for 4.2 miles. This road follows Buckskin Creek to the old Home Sweet Home Mine with its diggings and an abandoned brown building on the right. Park here. The road continues up to Kite Lake, but gets rougher past this point. Regular cars can easily come this far.

The Hike: Start northwest up the road and cross a small creek before reaching lovely Kite Lake in 1.4 miles from your vehicle. This is a popular spot for camping, and the trailhead for Mount Democrat. For Lake Emma, take the faint trail leading southwest from the toilet on the southern edge of Kite Lake. The trail gets faint at times and crosses the outflow of Lake Emma before steeply rising to the rocky lake, which will have some ice on the surface into July. Mount Democrat looms above to the north-northwest. Return as you ascended.

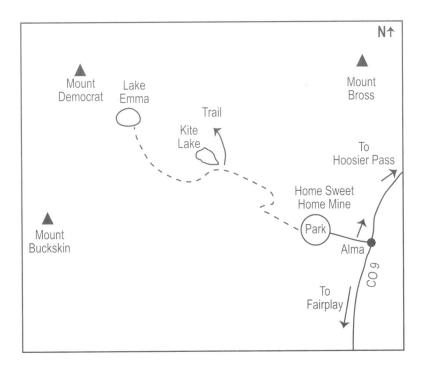

103 Heil Valley Ranch Loop

Hike Distance: 2.5 miles each way on Wapiti Trail, 2.6 miles on Ponderosa Loop, Total 7.6 miles

Hiking Time: Up on Wapiti Trail in 76 minutes. Ponderosa Loop in 69 minutes. Down Wapiti in 60 minut

Starting Elevation: 5,970 feet

Highest Elevation: 6,780 feet

Elevation Gain: 1,095 feet (includes 285 extra feet)

Trail: All the way

Relevant Maps: Trails Illustrated 100

Heil Valley Ranch (available at trailhead)

Lyons 7½ minute

Boulder County

Don't confuse the Heil Valley Ranch for its northern neighbor, the Hall Valley Ranch. Both are part of the North Foothills Open Space of Boulder. Dogs are not permitted in the park and bicycles can be used only on the Wapiti and Ponderosa Trails. This park is ideal for families, especially in the early and late hiking seasons.

Getting There: From the intersection with the Diagonal Highway (Iris Avenue) in Boulder, drive north on U.S. 36 for 7.2 miles. Then turn left onto Road 94, Lefthand Canyon, to Ward. After 0.6 mile from U.S. 36, turn right on Geer Canyon Drive. It is another 1.1 miles to the entrance of Heil Valley Ranch. Another 0.2 mile brings you past restrooms to parking at the main trailhead. There is no admission fee, and regular cars can reach this trailhead.

The Hike: Start out north-northwest on the Wapiti Trail. The Lichen Loop Trail on the right connects with the Wapiti Trail farther up the valley. After 0.7 mile take a left fork and pass through an open meadow. Cross a bridge and pass a bench before entering the forest. Soon pass a one-mile marker, and cross a dirt road. Shortly before the two-mile marker, pass a ruined stone dwelling on the right. At mile 2.5 you reach a signed fork and the beginning of the 2.6-mile Ponderosa Loop. Conical log piles have been present along the trail. At the far end of the Ponderosa Loop are two benches, some fencing, and a great overlook to the north. The top of Longs Peak can be seen to the west-northwest and Indian Head Mountain to the north. The Wild Turkey Trail connects on the east side of the two benches. Complete the Ponderosa Loop and return on the Wapiti Trail.

Group at Ponderosa Loop overlook

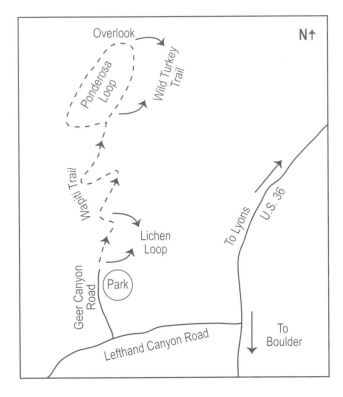

Mount Meeker and Longs Peak from high point of Hall Ranch Loop.

Hike Distance: 7.3 miles (total loop)

Hiking Time: 147 minutes total

Starting Elevation: 5,590 feet

Highest Elevation: 6,581 feet

Elevation Gain: 1,406 feet (includes 365 extra feet)

Trail: All the way

Relevant Maps: Trails Illustrated 100

   Hall Ranch (available at trailhead)

   Lyons 7½ minute

   Boulder County

   Roosevelt National Forest

The rolling hills of Hall Ranch offer several good trails, which have been well marked by the North Foothills Open Space. This keyhole loop takes you past the old Nelson Ranch House with good vistas to the north. Dogs are forbidden in Hall Ranch.

Getting There: From the south edge of Lyons, drive north (right) on U.S. 36 a few hundred yards and turn left onto Apple Valley Road. After less than a mile, turn left on Antelope Drive and park at the trailhead at the end of the road. This is an alternate trailhead; the main trailhead is just off CO 7 southwest of Lyons.

The Hike: Ascend southwest 1 mile to a sign and intersection. Continue to the right on the Bitterbrush Trail. After almost 1.6 miles on this clear main trail, reach a bench and a fork. This begins the Nelson Loop. For a counterclockwise route, take the right fork and ascend to a bench and a fork at the highest point of this hike. On clear days, Mount Meeker and Longs Peak can be seen to the northwest. The Nighthawk Trail continues straight, but to complete the Nelson Loop, descend left and soon pass the Nelson Ranch House on the left before completing the 2.2-mile loop and retracing your route back to the Antelope Trail and the trailhead.

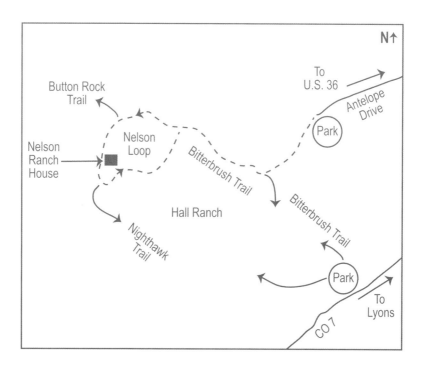

105 | Grizzly Lake

Many Colorado landmarks are named after the Grizzly, although they no longer reside in the state. The trail to Grizzly Lake begins near Buffalo Pass and is part of the Continental Divide Trail, which in this area is called the Wyoming Trail. The clear path meanders gradually over mostly level terrain with open meadows and wildflowers galore. Small, unspoiled Grizzly Lake is circled by high grass. This is a good family hike.

Getting There: Drive to Buffalo Pass on Road 60 north of Steamboat Springs. At the pass, drive south on Road 310 for 150 yards and turn left into the trailhead parking area. Regular cars can reach this point.

The Hike: Begin south on Trail 1101, the Wyoming Trail, and ascend through intermittent forest and meadow to a high point, before gradually descending under power lines. Occasional nearby lily ponds enrich the hike. Pass an unnamed small lake on the left before reaching a rock pile to the left of the trail and pristine Grizzly Lake 150 yards on your left. The Wyoming Trail continues southward. The return is gently upward most of the way and requires more stamina.

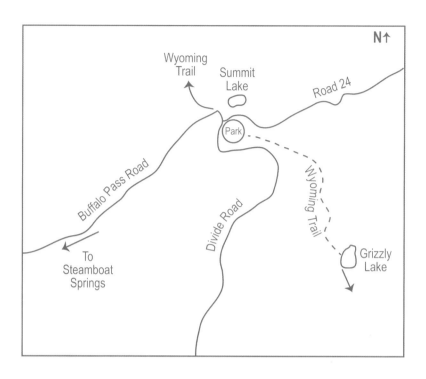

Hike Distance: 3.6 miles each way

Hiking Time: Out in 86 minutes. Back in 88 minutes.

Starting Elevation: 10,320 feet

Highest Elevation: 10,600 feet

Lowest Elevation: 10,202 feet (Grizzly Lake)

Elevation Gain: 1,008 feet (includes 728 extra feet)

Trail: All the way

Relevant Maps: Trails Illustrated 117

Buffalo Pass 7½ minute

Routt County Number Four

Jackson County Number Three

Routt National Forest

106 Alberta Peak

Hike Distance: 2.8 miles each way

Hiking Time: Up in 75 minutes. Down in 60 minutes.

Starting Elevation: 10,850 feet (Wolf Creek Pass)

Highest Elevation: 11,870 feet

Elevation Gain: 1,190 feet (includes 85 extra feet each way)

Trail: All the way except the last 0.1 mile before the summit

Relevant Maps: Trails Illustrated 140

Wolf Creek Pass 7½ minute

Archuleta County Number Three

San Juan National Forest

Views From the Summit: NNW to Wolf Creek Pass Ski Area

NE to Alberta Park Reservoir

WSW to Treasure Mountain

This hike uses the Continental Divide Trail and is infrequently used. The trail overlooks Wolf Creek Pass Ski Area to the east and north.

Getting There: Take U.S. 160 to Wolf Creek Pass, which is 35 miles west of Del Norte and 23 miles east of Pagosa Springs. Park off the road to the south near the Wolf Creek Pass sign.

The Hike: Begin south-southeast on the more easterly of two adjacent trails. Quickly cross a bridge and take the left fork and proceed south up into the trees. After 0.3 mile from the pass, take a right fork and keep on the west side of the ridge. Soon you will pass a large talus slope on your right and the first of two ski lifts on your left. In the upper grassy areas of the hike the trail is marked by the wooden poles of the Continental Divide Trail. Just west of the peak, the trail passes between two log structures. Just as the trail begins to descend on the south flank of Alberta Peak, leave the trail and ascend to the left (east) and traverse boulders to the top. The summit is marked by a pole in a cairn, a metal marker, and a small, excavated area. The Continental Divide Trail continues east to Railroad Pass and beyond. Return to Wolf Creek Pass as you ascended.

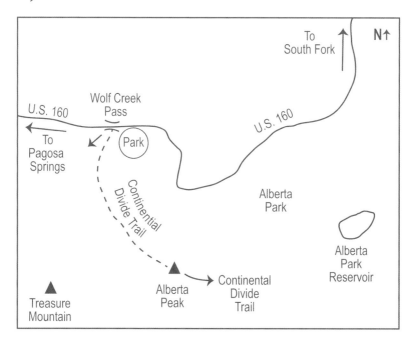

107 James Peak Lake and Little Echo Lake

Hike Distance: 6.0 miles total loop: Trailhead to James Peak Lake 2.5 miles, James Peak to Little Echo Lake 0.9 miles, Little Echo Lake to trailhead 2.6 miles

Hiking Time: 2.5 hours total; Trailhead to James Peak Lake in 60 minutes, James Peak to Little Echo Lake in 35 minutes, Little Echo Lake to trailhead in 55 minutes.

Starting Elevation: 11,180 feet

Highest Elevation: 11,570 feet

Elevation Gain: 1,305 feet (includes 208 extra feet)

Trail: All the way

Relevant Maps: Trails Illustrated 103

Empire 7½ minute

Gilpin County

Roosevelt National Forest

J ames Peak Lake and Little Echo Lake are surrounded by lovely scenery and reached by well-marked trails. Yet they lie in an out-of-the-way area and experience relatively little use. This route is mostly above timberline and the vistas are wonderful.

Getting There: From Rollinsville on CO 119, south of Nederland, drive west on the good, dirt Rollins Pass Road. Keep straight at mile 0.8 from CO 119, and at mile 5.1. Just past Tolland take the left fork up Mammoth Gulch. From Rollins Pass Road, keep straight at mile 0.1, left at the four-way intersection at mile 1.7, straight at mile 2.3, again at mile 3.6, and again at mile 4.8. Stay on Road 353. Take the right fork at mile 5.1 and park near the fork at mile 5.5. Regular cars should be able to come this far, but four-wheel drive is required past this point.

The Hike: From the parking area at the fork in the road, begin by going up the right fork in a westerly direction. After 1.4 miles on the rough road, you reach a sharp bend in the road to the left and the James Peak Trailhead sign. Descend this trail to the west-southwest and in 0.7 mile reach signs at the fork. The left trail leads to James Peak Lake and the right fork goes to Little Echo Lake and beyond to Rogers Pass on the Continental Divide. For this route description, go left past some tarns and waterfalls on your right and in 0.6 mile from the fork reach James Peak Lake with impressive James Peak above to the west-southwest. An abandoned cabin lies near the lake. To continue this hike return by the trail to the fork and descend left below timberline, cross the creek and then follow the trail up over tundra to serene Little Echo Lake. The trail continues along the right side of the lake and rises to the Continental Divide and beyond. Return back to the fork to James Peak Lake. Go left and ascend the 500 feet back to the road and the final 1.4 miles to reach your car.

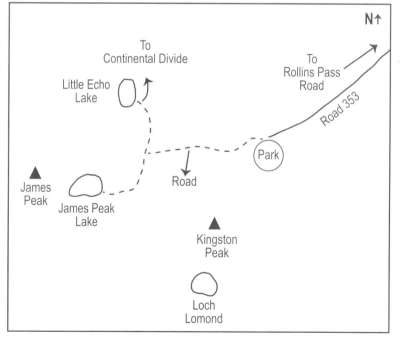

223

108 Hunt Lake

Trailhead to Hunt Lake

Hike Distance: 2.9 miles each way

Hiking Time: Up in 85 minutes. Down in 60 minutes.

Starting Elevation: 9,950 feet

Highest Elevation: 11,535 feet

Elevation Gain: 1,835 feet (includes 125 extra feet each way)

Trail: All the way

Relevant Maps: Trails Illustrated 130

Garfield 7½ minute

Chaffee County Number Three

San Isabel National Forest

L ying in the shadow of the Continental Divide, tranquil Hunt Lake is reached by a rough old mining road that uses part of the Continental Divide Trail. This area in lower Chaffee County is not heavily used. There are no restrictions on pets or bikes.

Getting There: Take U.S. 50 either west for 13.2 miles from the intersection with U.S. 285 west of Salida or east for 4.2 miles from Monarch Pass. Turn north on unpaved Forest Road 235. Drive 0.2 mile to a four-way intersection and park nearby off the road.

The Hike: Begin by going up the left fork (west) and ascend the rough four-wheel drive road (Road 235), which continues through the forest for 1.6 miles to a four-way intersection with the Boss Lake Reservoir below to the west. Take the left (south) fork on a road that is blocked to vehicles within 125 yards. Continue on the road, which is part of the Continental Divide Trail. The grade is moderate for the last 1.2 miles to Hunt Lake on the right. Shortly before reaching the lake, you pass an inviting meadow on the right. From Hunt Lake, Clover Mountain is the prominent peak to the northwest. Bald Mountain is to the west-southwest and Banana Mountain looms close above to the south. The trail continues up to the ridge and the Continental Divide.

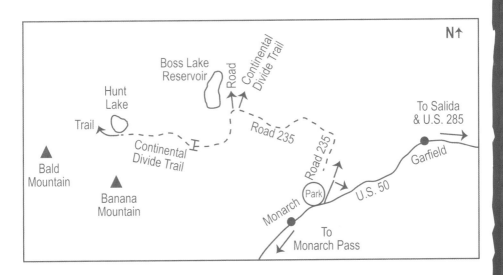

109 Prospect Mountain

Hike Distance: 2.6 miles each way

Hiking Time: Up in 82 minutes. Down in 60 minutes.

Starting Elevation: 11,205 feet

Highest Elevation: 12,614 feet

Elevation Gain: 1,419 feet (includes 5 extra feet each way)

Trail: Initial 0.8 mile only

Relevant Maps: Trails Illustrated 109 or 149

    Climax 7½ minute

    Lake County

    San Isabel National Forest

Views From the Summit: N to Jaque Peak

    NNE to Mount Arkansas

    NE to Treasurevault Mountain, Mosquito Peak

    ENE to Mosquito Pass

    ESE to Mount Evans

    S to Mount Harvard

    SE to Gemini Peak, Mount Sherman, Dyer Mountain

    SW to Leadville, Mount Hope, La Plata Peak, Mount Elbert

    W to Homestake Peak

    WNW to Mount of the Holy Cross

    WSW to Turquoise Lake, Mount Massive

P rospect Mountain overlooks Leadville and is covered with old mining artifacts. The easiest access to the summit is this route from Mosquito Pass Road.

Getting There: From Harrison Avenue in the center of Leadville, drive east on East Seventh Street. Keep left after 2.8 miles and park at a fork and a metal Mosquito Pass sign 4.2 miles from Harrison Avenue. The road up Mosquito Pass gets rougher beyond this point. Regular cars can come this far.

The Hike: Begin by taking the left fork and proceeding north-northeast. Soon take another left fork at a sign describing the Diamond Mine. Descend a little and then ascend the Mosquito Pass Road leading northeast. Leave the road 0.5 mile from the trailhead and ascend north-northwest (left) over tundra. Eventually pass over some talus and keep to the left side of the bald subpeak to reach a saddle directly north of Lake Isabelle, which will be visible to your left. Ascend gradually west from the saddle to a cairn atop the flat summit of Prospect Mountain. The best return is to retrace your ascent route and thereby avoid going through heavier forest.

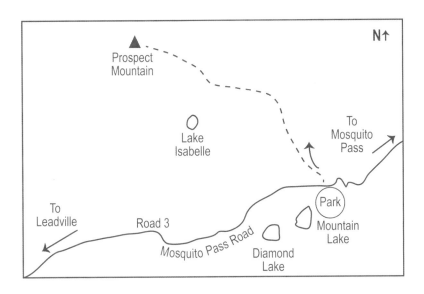

110 Scott Gomer Creek Beaver Ponds

When the aspen leaves turn to gold in the second half of each September, many hikers want a trail in the midst of this autumn splendor. Of the many good aspen hikes in Colorado, this one along Scott Gomer Creek in the Mount Evans Wilderness, with several water crossings, abounds with golden leaves and is one of the best.

Getting There: Drive north from U.S. 285 at Grant on Park County Road 62 for 5.0 miles or drive south from Guanella Pass on Road 62 for 7.7 miles. Park in a large area on the east at Burning Bear Trailhead. Regular cars can reach this point.

The Hike: Begin north through an open gate and pass by a signboard and trail register. Follow the clear, rocky, Abyss Lake Trail as it gradually ascends the valley, crosses the creek, and breaks out into the open after 2.1 miles. Continue up the valley on the main trail with Mount Bierstadt and Mount Evans, two fourteeners, looming ahead. Just before reaching a signed trail fork, which is your turnaround point, there is a meadow on the right with many beaver ponds. Enjoy the colorful surroundings. From the fork, the Abyss Lake Trail continues to the left and joins the Rosalie Trail that enters from the right.

Hike Distance: 3.8 miles each way

Hiking Time: Up in 105 minutes. Down in 90 minutes.

Starting Elevation: 9,630 feet

Highest Elevation: 10,600 feet

Elevation Gain: 1,150 feet (includes 90 extra feet each way)

Trail: All the way

Relevant Maps: Trails Illustrated 104

Mount Evans 7½ minute

Park County Number Two

Pike National Forest

Scott Gomer Creek Beaver Ponds

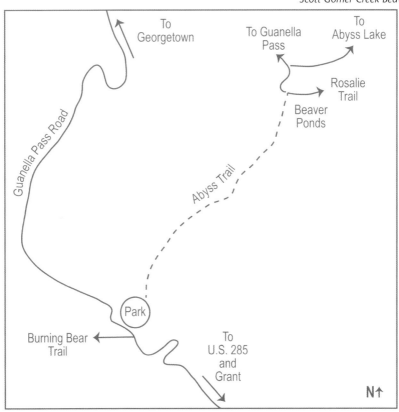

To Georgetown

To Guanella Pass

To Abyss Lake

Rosalie Trail

Beaver Ponds

Guanella Pass Road

Abyss Trail

Park

Burning Bear Trail

To U.S. 285 and Grant

N↑

229

111 Hartenstein Lake

S cenic Buena Vista is a great central point from which many good hikes originate. This one leads to a lake in the Collegiate Peaks Wilderness with Mount Yale looming above to the northeast. The lake is named after George K. Hartenstein, a Buena Vista attorney at the turn of the century.

Getting There: From Main Street in Buena Vista, which is U.S. 24, drive west at the stoplight on Chaffee County 306 for 12.3 miles to the paved Denny Creek Trailhead parking area on your right. Park here. Denny Creek lies just to the east. (This road continues west over Cottonwood Pass to Taylor Park and Crested Butte.)

The Hike: Begin northwest up from the Denny Creek Trailhead. After 1 mile the first of the two creek crossings occurs. The trail turns west and at mile 2.0 a fork and sign are reached. Go left (south-southwest), cross the creek again and follow the trail as it winds clockwise around a small hill to reach Hartenstein Lake from its north side in another mile from the fork. The right fork leads up to Browns Pass, 1.5 miles, and beyond to Kroenke Lake, 3.5 miles.

Hike Distance: 3.0 miles each way

Hiking Time: Up in 96 minutes. Down in 72 minutes.

Starting Elevation: 9,900 feet

Highest Elevation: 11,451 feet

Elevation Gain: 1,711 feet (includes 80 extra feet each way)

Trail: All the way

Relevant Maps: Trails Illustrated 129 or 148

   Mount Yale 7½ minute

   Chaffee County Number Two

   San Isabel National Forest

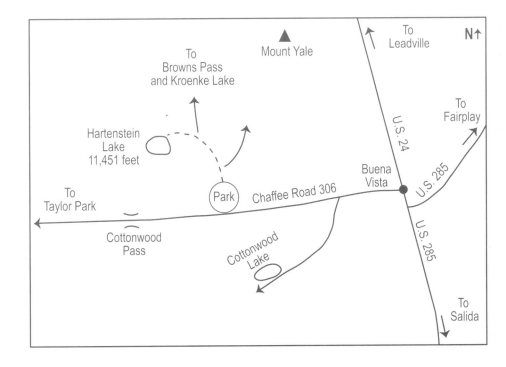

112 Boreas Mountain

The hike to Boreas Mountain begins at Boreas Pass and several cabins and historic informational signs. There is no trail. Avoid the willows in your ascent to the ridge over tundra and rocks. Around the summit lies a myriad of orange talus. Boreas was the ancient Greek God of the North Wind.

Getting There: From CO 9 at the south end of Breckenridge, drive east on the Boreas Pass Road (Road 10) 10.3 miles and park at the pass. From U.S. 285 at Como, Road 33 also reaches the pass.

The Hike: Begin to the northeast and reach tree line after 0.5 mile. Then curve to the east and find your route to the high point. A register and rock shelter mark the Boreas Mountain summit. Relish the moment before avoiding the steeper rocks back to Boreas Pass.

Mount Guyot from Boreas Mountain

Hike Distance: 2.3 miles each way

Hiking Time: Up in 87 minutes. Down in 59 minutes.

Starting Elevation: 11,481 feet

Highest Elevation: 13,082 feet

Elevation Gain: 1,621 feet (includes 10 extra feet each way)

Trail: None

Relevant Maps: Trails Illustrated 109

    Boreas Pass 7½ minute

    Park County Number One

    Pike National Forest

Views From the Summit: N to Mount Guyot

    NNE to Mount Bierstadt, Mount Evans

    NNW to Bald Mountain

    NW to Peak 8

    E to North Twin Cone Peak

    S to Buffalo Peaks

    SSW to Mount Silverheels

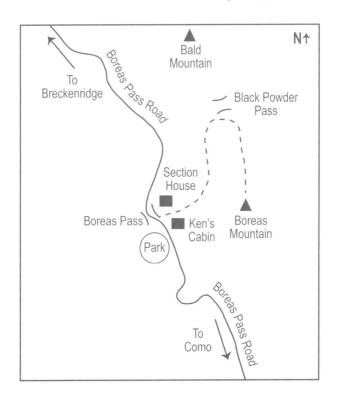

113 Independence Lake and Lost Man Pass

Lost Man Lake from Lost Man Pass

This hike originates from the first switchback west of Independence Pass, enters the Hunter-Fryingpan Wilderness, and proceeds mostly above timberline to the north past tranquil Independence Lake to unofficially named Lost Man Pass.

Getting There: Drive on CO 82 either 1.8 miles west and north from Independence Pass or 17.9 miles east from the center of Aspen at Mill Street and Main Street, which is CO 82. Park off the road to the north by the trailhead.

The Hike: Start to the north-northwest at a sign and trail register. Follow the Lost Man Trail, and in 0.25 mile keep right at a fork and a trail sign. Cross the Roaring Fork River, which originates in this basin. Pass over tundra and reach Independence Lake in 2 miles from the trailhead. Continue north to the left of the lake another 0.4 mile to Lost Man Pass. East Geissler Mountain lies to the left (west) and several unnamed peaks lie ahead and up to the right along the Continental Divide. The Lost Man Trail continues from the pass down to the north past Lost Man Lake, around to the northwest and then south back to CO 82. For this hike, return to the south as you ascended.

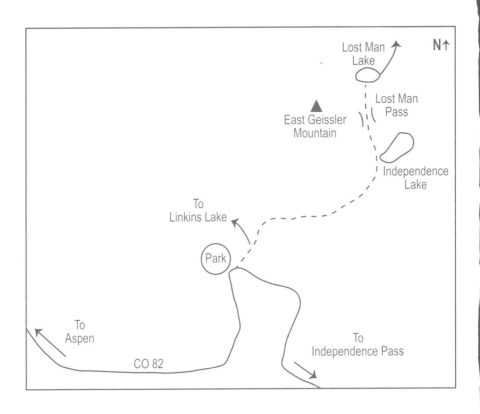

Hike Distance: 2.4 miles each way

Hiking Time: Up in 69 minutes. Down in 50 minutes.

Starting Elevation: 11,506 feet

Highest Elevation: 12,820 feet (Lost Man Pass)

Elevation Gain: 1,358 feet (includes 22 extra feet each way)

Trail: All the way

Relevant Maps: Trails Illustrated 127 or 148

   Independence Pass 7½ minute

   Mount Champion 7½ minute

   Pitkin County Number Two

   White River National Forest

114 Mount Sniktau

Closeness to the Front Range and the high starting point makes Mount Sniktau a popular hike. Perhaps nowhere else in Colorado can you hike so high so quickly. Sniktau was a pen name used by E.H.N. Patterson, a Clear Creek County journalist of the mid-1800s.

Getting There: Drive on U.S. 6 to Loveland Pass either from I-70 at Exit 216 just before the Eisenhower–Johnson Tunnel on the east or from Keystone on the west. Park off the east side of the pass.

The Hike: Begin to the east and follow the clear, steep trail up over a series of grass and rock benches to the ridge. Continue left (north) to a false summit with two rock piles. Descend north to a saddle and follow the trail up to a benchmark, rock pile, and extraordinary views in every direction.

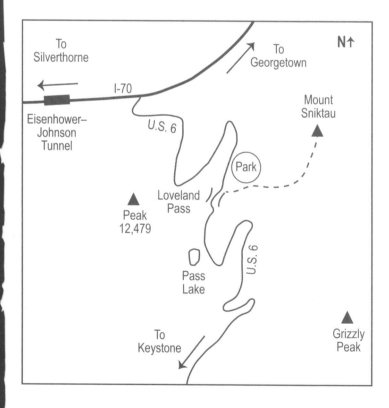

Hike Distance: 2.4 miles each way

Hiking Time: Up in 90 minutes. Down in 68 minutes.

Starting Elevation: 11,990 feet (Loveland Pass)

Highest Elevation: 13,234 feet

Elevation Gain: 1,670 feet (includes 213 extra feet each way)

Trail: All the way

Relevant Maps: Trails Illustrated 104

    Loveland Pass 7½ minute

    Grays Peak 7½ minute

    Clear Creek County

    Arapaho National Forest

Views From the Summit: N to Mount Machebeuf

    NNE to Longs Peak, Mount Parnassus, Bard Peak

    NW to Pettingell Peak, Mount Bethel

    SSE to Grizzly Peak

    SE to Torreys Peak, Grays Peak

    SW to Mount of the Holy Cross, Buffalo Mountain

    WNW to Hagar Mountain

    WSW to Mount Powell

115 Ptarmigan Lake

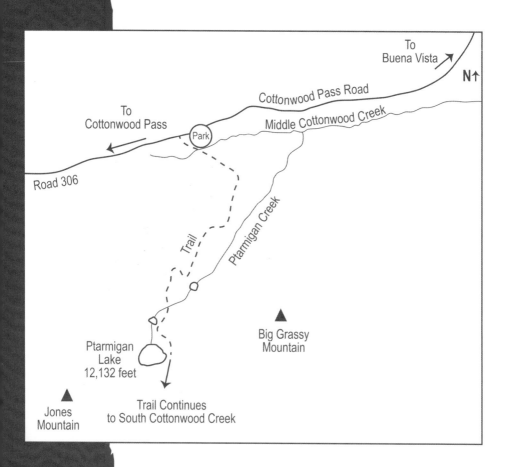

To Buena Vista

N↑

Cottonwood Pass Road

To Cottonwood Pass

Middle Cottonwood Creek

Park

Road 306

Trail

Ptarmigan Creek

Big Grassy Mountain

Ptarmigan Lake
12,132 feet

Jones Mountain

Trail Continues
to South Cottonwood Creek

If you have never been to Buena Vista, you owe yourself a trip to this mountain haven. There are numerous trails, lakes, and mountains on public land and the Collegiate Peaks, a group of fourteeners, loom above the town to the west. The hike to Ptarmigan Lake puts you in the middle of this playground.

Getting There: From the stop light in Buena Vista at the junction of U.S. 24 and Main Street, drive west on Chaffee County Road 306 for 14.7 miles toward Cottonwood Pass. Turn left at a sign and park at the end of the road and trailhead within 200 yards of Cottonwood Pass Road.

The Hike: Begin by descending a bit to the south-southeast on the trail. Pass a trail register and cross a bridge over Middle Cottonwood Creek. Soon you traverse a talus and boulder slope. Proceed generally upward to the south and through the trees on a clear trail. In a little over a mile from the trailhead, cross a logging road and follow the trail south at a sign. There has been much logging in the middle part of this hike. Follow a switchback to the northeast shortly after crossing the road and eventually arrive at a meadow. A small pool will be present soon on your right and an unnamed lake down on your left. On the final ascent above timberline another unnamed lake will be seen to your right. At larger Ptarmigan Lake there is a sign and lots of tundra. Mount Yale can be seen to the north-northeast, Jones Mountain to the southwest, and Big Grassy Mountain dominating the eastern horizon. The trail continues south down into the South Cottonwood Creek drainage, but your return will be by your ascent route.

Hike Distance: 3.1 miles each way

Hiking Time: Up in 85 minutes. Down in 74 minutes.

Starting Elevation: 10,655 feet

Highest Elevation: 12,132 feet

Elevation Gain: 1,557 feet (includes 40 extra feet each way)

Trail: All the way

Relevant Maps: Trails Illustrated 129 or 148

Tincup 7½ minute

Mount Yale 7½ minute

Chaffee County Number Two

San Isabel National Forest

116 Slide Lake

Slide Lake and Homestake Peak

Hike Distance: 3.4 miles each way

Hiking Time: Up in 88 minutes. Down in 76 minutes.

Starting Elevation: 10,590 feet

Highest Elevation: 11,710 feet

Elevation Gain: 1,370 feet (includes 125 extra feet each way)

Trail: All the way

Relevant Maps: Trails Illustrated 109 and 126, or 149

   Homestake Reservoir 7½ minute

   Leadville North 7½ minute

   Lake County

   San Isabel National Forest

f you like to get away from other people in the out-of-doors, this hike within the Holy Cross Wilderness is for you. The route follows an old mining road up to a calm lake at the foot of Homestake Peak. There are lovely meadows on your left as you near the lake. These would make great campsites. There is even a picnic table along the trail 0.25 mile before the lake.

Getting There: From its intersection with CO 91 just north of Leadville, drive north on U.S. 24 for 7.1 miles and turn left onto a dirt road. This turnoff is 1.6 miles south of Tennessee Pass. Follow the good main road and keep left at 0.3 mile, right at 0.9 mile and left at 1.6 miles from U.S. 24. Pass a cabin on your left and be sure to stay on the left side of the drainage canal, known as Wurts Ditch. At mile 1.7, just past the cabin, park around a fence off the road. Four-wheel drive would be required beyond this point.

The Hike: Start walking north and follow the road by passing around the barrier to vehicles. The road turns west and rises and falls through the forest before breaking out into a series of lovely green clearings. Blue diamond tree blazes mark the road, which is your trail. The Continental Divide is on your right throughout the entire ascent.

At 2.9 miles from the starting point, a road descends left to reach the 10th Mountain Division Hut, which can be rented for overnight use. (Call 970-925-5775 for information.) Continue straight, however, for the final 0.5 mile to the lake, pass a picnic table on the left and a trail register shortly thereafter. Cross the outflow creek from Slide Lake and hike past a wilderness sign before reaching the large lake around timberline with Homestake Peak beyond to the southwest.

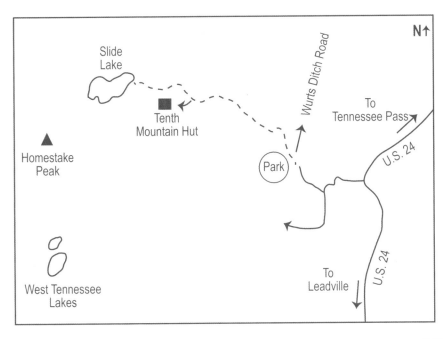

241

117 Lyle Lake and Mormon Lake

Trailhead to Lyle Lake

Lyle and Mormon Lakes are located in a remote area of the Holy Cross Wilderness. Their beauty and the surrounding grandeur make them worthwhile hiking destinations.

Getting There: These lakes are reached from Hagerman Pass Road. The easiest vehicular access is from the west. Drive east from CO 82 between Glenwood Springs and Aspen through Basalt and past the Ruedi Reservoir. Get on Road 105 and from a signed fork, with the left road leading to Diemer Lake and Sellar Lake, drive the right fork (Road 105), Hagerman Pass Road, for 7.4 more miles to a four-way intersection. The right fork leads to Ivanhoe Lake. Road 105 continues straight and becomes more rough. In another 0.1 mile the trailhead and a small parking area lay on the left. Access from the east requires a four-wheel-drive vehicle with high clearance. The trailhead lies 3.8 miles west of Hagerman Pass. From the west, regular cars can reach the four-way intersection just before the trailhead.

The Hike: Begin northeast from the trailhead sign and register. Ascend gradually through mostly open meadow for 1.5 miles to scenic Lyle Lake. The rounded, grassy summit of Lyle Peak can be seen to the southeast. A faint trail surrounds the lake. The western side is grassy and the eastern side is rocky. Continue to the far end of the lake and ascend a steeper trail to the north-northeast. After reaching the high point of this hike you will gradually descend by trail and occasional cairns. The trail passes below cliffs and boulders on the right and then briefly enters the trees. The final segment before Mormon Lake passes through lovely open tundra and alongside a small pond before a gentle descent to the north-northeast. The trail gets faint and ends near the lake. A rocky wall lies behind Mormon Lake with gentler slopes above to the right. Return as you came. Use your compass and don't lose the trail.

Hike Distance: 3.3 miles each way
(1.5 miles to Lyle Lake, 1.8 miles to Mormon Lake)

Hiking Time: Up to Lyle Lake in 40 minutes and an
additional 55 minutes to Mormon Lake.
Down in 75 minutes.

Starting Elevation: 10,720 feet

Highest Elevation: 11,680 feet

Elevation Gain: 1,670 feet
(includes 710 extra feet)

Trail: All the way

Relevant Maps: Trails Illustrated 126 or 149

Nast 7½ minute

Pitkin County Number Two

White River National Forest

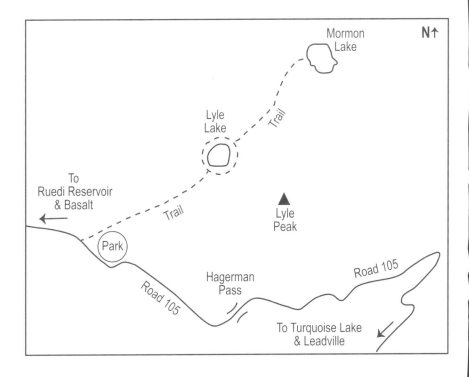

118 Lower Blue Lake

O f all the blue lakes in Colorado, this may be the bluest. Lying below Mount Sneffels, the setting is spectacular in the Mount Sneffels Wilderness. The trail continues up to the Middle and Upper Blue Lakes.

Getting There: From CO 62 between Ridgeway and Placerville drive south on Dallas Creek Road (Ouray 7) for 8.8 miles to the Blue Lakes Trailhead. En route keep left at mile 0.3 and at mile 1.6. Go right at mile 2.0 and at mile 7.1. At mile 8.7 go straight into the trailhead parking area.

The Hike: Start to the south and quickly take the right fork near a trail register. The left fork is the Blaine Basin Trail. At around 2 miles from the trailhead, pass a wilderness sign and a little farther, cross a creek. Continue up into the vast basin and enjoy your arrival at Lower Blue Lake and its striking color. The route to the higher lakes leads to the left.

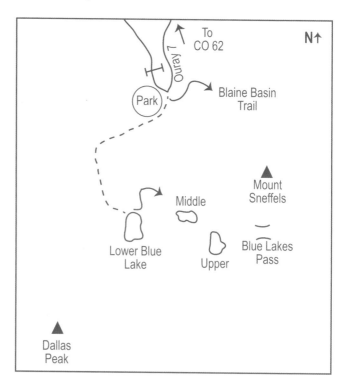

Group at Lower Blue Lake

Hike Distance: 3.3 miles each way

Hiking Time: Up in 116 minutes. Down in 85 minutes

Starting Elevation: 9,400 feet

Highest Elevation: 10,980 feet

Elevation Gain: 2,168 feet (includes 294 extra feet each way)

Trail: All the way

Relevant Maps: Trails Illustrated 141

    Mount Sneffels 7½ minute

    Ouray County Number Two

    Uncompahgre National Forest

119 Steuart Lake and Reynolds Lake Loop

Steuart Lake and Mount Bancroft

Hike Distance: Up in 4.1 miles. Down in 2.9 miles (total 7.0 miles)

Hiking Time: Up in 110 minutes. Down in 66 minutes.

Starting Elevation: 10,560 feet

Highest Elevation: 11,700 feet

Elevation Gain: 1,295 feet (includes 155 extra feet)

Trail: Initial 85% and some of final 5% (on counterclockwise ascent); 100% on descent.

Relevant Maps: Trails Illustrated 103

Empire 7½ mile

Clear Creek County

Arapaho National Forest

The Continental Divide Trail leads up, steeply at times, to tundra and great vistas above tree line. After leaving the trail you will reach two of the five lakes that lie above Loch Lomond.

Getting There: Take Exit 238 from I-70 west of Idaho Springs. Drive up Fall River Road 8 miles and turn left onto Alice Road. Keep on this road 0.9 mile, then turn right on the rough road at the junction. High clearance will be needed for about 0.6 mile until you park at a crossing of the Continental Divide Trail.

The Hike: Begin up the trail north-northwest as it rises steeply to tree line where the scenery is magnificent. Continue across an old road and pass a wilderness sign. At a clump of trees on the left of the trail, leave the trail and proceed on a level grade southwest to the ridge. En route, cross a trail and reach a faint trail below the ridge leading down to the lakes. The trail fades away but the walk to Steuart Lake is easy. From this lake, hike left and find a trail that crosses a dam and passes by Reynolds Lake on the right. Mount Bancroft towers above both lakes. The trail then descends steeply and runs along the right side of Loch Lomond. Old pipes run alongside some of the trail. From Loch Lomond follow the wide road down the valley to your starting point.

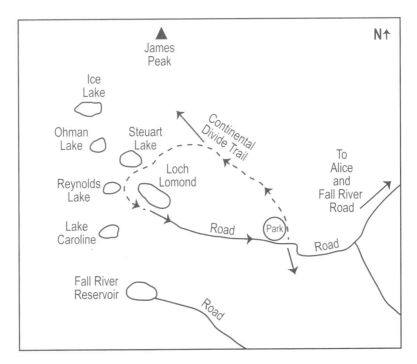

Lower Chicago Lake

Hike Distance: 3.5 miles each way

Hiking Time: Out in 135 minutes. Back in 115 minutes.

Starting Elevation: 10,680 feet

Highest Elevation: 11,510 feet

Lowest Elevation: 10,360 feet

Elevation Gain: 1,572 feet (includes 742 extra feet)

Trail: All the way

Relevant Maps: Trails Illustrated 104

    Idaho Springs 7½ minute

    Mount Evans 7½ minute

    Clear Creek County

    Arapaho National Forest

Lower Chicago Lake from the south

L ocated in a rocky bowl in the Mount Evans Wilderness, Lower Chicago Lake is a scenic destination. Bicycles and motorized vehicles are forbidden in the wilderness area. The second half of this hike to Lower Chicago Lake is more difficult, as is the second half on your return route. The rocky peaks above make this an especially scenic setting at the lower lake.

Getting There: From Idaho Springs drive south from I-70 (Exit 240) on CO 103 for 13.1 miles and turn right onto CO 5. Park on the left just before the gate on Mount Evans Road. Another access is 18 miles from CO 74 at Bergen Park on CO 103.

The Hike: Start out to the west from the trail sign 50 feet beyond the road gate. Follow this good trail with Echo Lake on the right 0.5 mile to a signed fork. Go left and rise to a shelf trail that descends to a crossing of Chicago Creek and a road. Continue up steeply to the left. Pass the Idaho Springs Reservoir and two cabins as the trail curves right and enters the Mount Evans Wilderness at signs and a register. The trail becomes steeper and passes to the left of an old burn area and huge boulder en route to the highest point of this outing. A small creek crossing occurs before you emerge from the forest with Lower Chicago Lake 80 feet below the trail on the left. The trail continues to Upper Chicago Lake and the trail that crosses Mount Spalding and leads to the top of Mount Evans. Enjoy the beauty before your return and the demanding final 1.5 miles back to the trailhead.

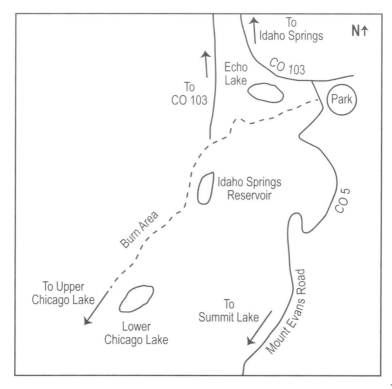

121 Highland Mary Lakes

The Highland Mary Lakes are several and lie within the Weminuche Wilderness. A good trail takes you up to two separate basins and wonderful vistas.

Getting There: From central Silverton, drive east on San Juan Road Two 4.2 miles to Howardsville. Turn right on County Road 4 and proceed up Cunningham Gulch 4.7 more miles. Park at road end at the trailhead sign and register. En route to this point keep right 1.7 miles from Howardsville and avoid the road to Stony Pass. Four-wheel drive will be required for the final mile to the trailhead.

The Hike: Start out up to the south. The initial going is steep. Keep right at a sign, pass a creek, and follow the clear, main trail up over a ridge. Descend slightly before the trail rises to a shelf trail that leads to an open basin with a small lake. Cross a boulder field and regain the trail that rises to a higher basin with two larger Highland Mary Lakes. Enjoy and refresh before returning as you came.

Hike Distance: 3.2 miles each way

Hiking Time: Up in 98 minutes. Down in 70 minutes.

Starting Elevation: 10,400 feet

Highest Elevation: 12,100 feet

Elevation Gain: 1,866 feet (includes 166 extra feet)

Trail: All the way

Relevant Maps: Trails Illustrated 141

Howardsville 7½ minute

San Juan County

San Juan National Forest

One of the Highland Mary Lakes

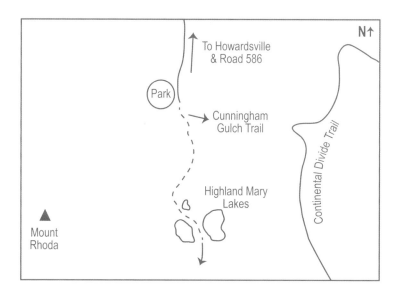

122 Glacier Peak

Beginning at Georgia Pass, the hike to Glacier Peak traverses the Continental Divide and provides lovely vistas. The route uses an old mining road part of the way and is largely above timberline. The Georgia Pass Road from the South Park side is surprisingly easy to negotiate.

Getting There: At Jefferson in South Park drive northwest from U.S. 285 on the National Forest road. Avoid the right fork at mile 2. Turn right at mile 2.9 on Road 54. Keep on the main road. Go left at mile 5.3 and reach Georgia Pass at mile 12 and park. Regular cars with reasonable clearance can reach Georgia Pass from South Park. However, the access from CO 9 north of Breckenridge is a difficult four-wheel-drive road.

The Hike: Begin on foot up the old rough road to the north. In less than 0.5 mile, cross the Colorado Trail and continue up the road to a four-way intersection. Continue straight (north-northeast) on a road, which is now closed to motor vehicles by a fence. Ascend the ridge after passing through the fence. Cross two subpeaks on Glacier Ridge and continue up the road. Keep right at a fork at the base of the peak. A ridge is reached at mile 2.8. Leave the road here and ascend right (east-southeast) over tundra for the final 0.1 mile to a pole, a rock pile, and a USGS benchmark at the top of Glacier Peak. A subpeak lies to the east as does Whale Peak, another 1.5 miles along the Divide. The easiest return from Glacier Peak descends directly south to the old road and then back as you ascended.

Hike Distance: 2.9 miles each way

Hiking Time: Up in 77 minutes. Down in 65 minutes.

Starting Elevation: 11,585 feet (Georgia Pass)

Highest Elevation: 12,853 feet

Elevation Gain: 1,534 feet (includes 133 extra feet each way)

Trail: All the way until the final 150 yards

Relevant Maps: Trails Illustrated 109

> Boreas Pass 7½ minute

> Park County Number One

> Pike National Forest

Views From the Summit: N to Torreys Peak, Grays Peak

> NE to Whale Peak

> S to Buffalo Peaks

> SSW to Mount Silverheels

> SW to Mount Guyot

> WSW to Peak 8, Mount of the Holy Cross

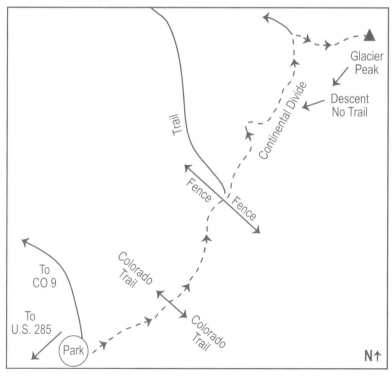

123 Nolan Lake

How about a picnic at Nolan Lake beneath impressive Gold Dust Peak? This lovely hike is all it takes. Named after William Nolan, an early Fulford prospector, the lake is reached by a good trail that passes through the remnants of the upper town of Fulford and several clearings before passing by a waterfall of Nolan Creek and then curving clockwise to ascend to the lake.

Getting There: From I-70, between Glenwood Springs and Vail, take Exit 147 and drive south to Eagle. Turn left onto Broadway in Eagle and follow the signs to Sylvan Lake. Once you get on Brush Creek Road, which eventually crosses Crooked Creek Pass and descends to Fryingpan Road, east of the Ruedi Reservoir, drive 10.8 miles south from Eagle on Brush Creek Road. Turn left just before a bridge and follow the good, dirt road along East Brush Creek to Fulford. From Brush Creek Road, stay on the main road, keep straight at mile 4.2 and again at mile 5.9. Take a left fork at mile 6.2, go right at mile 6.9, and left at mile 7. Go straight at mile 8.7 and reach a fork with Fulford on the left at mile 9.9. Nolan Creek passes under the road here and the trailhead for Nolan Lake is 30 feet ahead on the right. Park off the road.

The Hike: Start walking southeast up the rough road, which is blocked to car traffic. A register lies on the left. After passing through the old upper town, the trail reaches a fork. A sign directs you up to the left. Go right at an ensuing fork at another sign. The trail meanders through lovely terrain, passes some talus and boulders on the left and later a waterfall on the right. After entering the Holy Cross Wilderness, you reach a lovely meadow. Another sign directs you up a steeper segment to finally reach Nolan Lake over a bluff at 11,260 feet. The trail continues along the right side of the lake to the northwest to reach a large boulder at the edge of the lake, which provides a great overlook back toward Fulford and beyond to the northwest. Gold Dust Peak looms above to the southeast, Craig Peak to the west, and New York Mountain to the north-northwest. Revel in the natural beauty and return as you ascended.

Hike Distance: 3.5 miles each way

Hiking Time: Up in 106 minutes. Down in 82 minutes.

Starting Elevation: 9,920 feet

Highest Elevation: 11,342 feet

Elevation Gain: 1,996 feet (includes 574 extra feet)

Trail: All the way

Relevant Maps: Trails Illustrated 121 and 126 or 149

    Fulford Pass 7½ minute

    Crooked Creek Pass 7½ minute

    Mount Jackson 7½ minute

    Eagle County Number Three

    White River National Forest

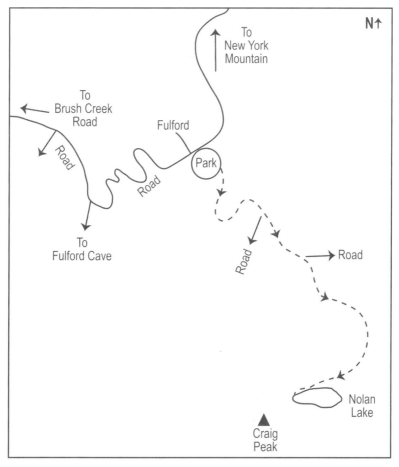

124 Lyle Peak

Lyle Peak lies on the Continental Divide and within the Holy Cross Wilderness. Great vistas are abundant from the Divide above tree line.

Getting There: From Turquoise Lake Road on the south side of Turquoise Lake take Hagerman Pass Road for 7.8 miles to the pass and park near the pass sign. Vehicles with good clearance can reach the pass. Hagerman Pass can also be reached from CO 82, Basalt and the Ruedi Reservoir to the west.

The Hike: Lyle Peak is visible from Hagerman Pass. Begin to the northwest and lose some elevation. Continue northwest and pass through some trees with Divide Peak on the right. Gain the ridge and a faint trail. Descend to a saddle and pass under power lines. Ascend the tundra to a benchmark and cairn at the Lyle Peak high point. Return south on the ascent route.

Lyle Lake from Lyle Peak

Hike Distance: 3.0 miles each way

Hiking Time: Up in 93 minutes. Down in 85 minutes.

Starting Elevation: 11,925 feet (Hagerman Pass)

Highest Elevation: 12,489 feet

Lowest Elevation: 11,760 feet

Elevation Gain: 1,004 feet (includes 275 extra feet)

Trail: none, except occasional faint trail along the Continental Divide

Relevant Maps: Trails Illustrated 126 or 149

Homestake Reservoir 7½ minute

Nast 7½ minute

Pitkin County Number Two

White River National Forest

Views From the Summit: N to Mount of the Holy Cross

NNE to Galena Mountain

NW to Lyle Lake

ENE to Timberline Lake

ESE to Turquoise Lake

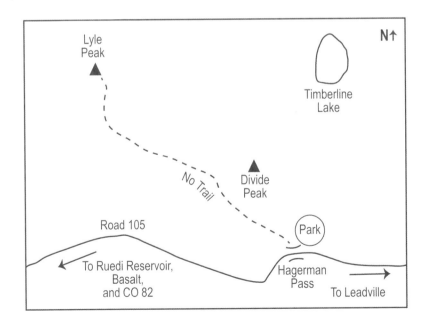

125 Epaulet Mountain and Rosalie Peak

Hike Distance: 3.1 miles each way

Hiking Time: Up to Epaulet Mountain in 43 minutes.
Over to Rosalie Peak in 48 minutes. Down in 84 minutes.

Starting Elevation: 13,250 feet (Mount Evans Road)

Highest Elevation: 13,575 feet

Elevation Gain: 940 feet (includes 715 extra feet)

Trail: None

Relevant Maps: Trails Illustrated 104

    Mount Evans 7½ minute

    Harris Park 7½ minute

    Clear Creek County

    Park County

    Arapaho National Forest

Views From the Summits:

    Epaulet Mountain: N to Rogers Peak

        NNE to Chief Mountain, Squaw Peak

        NNW to Longs Peak, Mount Meeker

        NW to Mount Evans

        SSE to Mount Logan

        ESE to Rosalie Peak

        W to Mount Bierstadt

    Rosalie Peak: N to Longs Peak, Mount Meeker

        NW to Mount Evans

        SSE to Pikes Peak

        SW to Mount Silverheels, Kataka Mountain

        S to Mount Logan

        WNW to Mount Bierstadt, the Sawtooth, Epaulet Mountain

Rosalie and Epaulet from Mount Logan

The hike to these two mid-thirteeners lies in the Mount Evans Wilderness and is totally above tree line. There is no trail but the footing is good over tundra and rock. With no tree obstruction the scenery is magnificent.

Getting There: From the intersection of CO 103 and CO 5 (Mount Evans Road), drive up past the fee station for 10.8 miles and park off the road in a level area on the left. This point is shortly before the road curves sharply up to the right.

The Hike: Begin with a slight descent to the south and then head directly for Epaulet Mountain. There is no summit marker. Continue down steeply to the southeast and reach a broad saddle. Ascend Rosalie Peak to the southeast and keep slightly to the right of a bluff en route to a rock pile and a register. For the return, descend back to the saddle and then angle along the right side of Epaulet Mountain and avoid its summit, as well as some steep drop-offs also on the right.

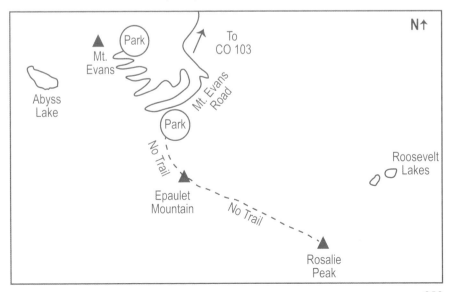

126 Geneva Mountain

Starting from Guanella Pass, the hike to Geneva Mountain is totally above timberline, with great scenery. Geneva Mountain is not to be confused with Geneva Peak, which lies north of Webster Pass, farther southwest in Park County. Guanella Pass is named after Byron Guanella, a former Clear Creek County Commissioner, who promoted work on the pass.

Getting There: Drive to Guanella Pass, which connects Grant and U.S. 285 from the south with Georgetown and I-70 on the north. Park in the large area on the east. Regular cars can traverse the pass from the north or the south.

The Hike: Begin on foot to the south from the Rosalie Trailhead. After 200 yards, take a left (east) fork. Follow the old road another mile to a signed fork. The Rosalie Trail goes left and descends into the valley, but continue straight (south-southeast). Follow the dirt road, which is faint at times, until it ascends an unnamed peak. Leave the trail halfway up and veer left (south) across rock and tundra. Continue over two false summits before reaching the high point at the southern edge of the ridge. A modest rock pile marks the summit. Enjoy a scenic respite before retracing your route back to the north-northwest.

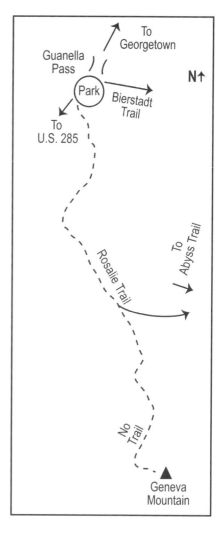

Hikers on Geneva Mountain with Mount Bierstadt in the background

Hike Distance: 3.5 miles each way

Hike Time: Up in 88 minutes. Down in 86 minutes.

Starting Elevation: 11,669 feet (Guanella Pass)

Highest Elevation: 12,335 feet

Elevation Gain: 1,636 feet (includes 485 extra feet each way)

Trail: First Half

Relevant Maps: Trails Illustrated 104

    Mount Evans 7½ minute

    Clear Creek County

    Park County Number Two

    Pike National Forest

Views From the Summit: NNE to Mount Bierstadt, Mount Evans

    SSE to North Twin Cone Peak

    SE to Mount Logan

    SW to Mount Silverheels

    WNW to Square Top Mountain

127 Heart Lake and Rogers Pass Lake

Heart Lake from Rogers Pass

Heart Lake and Rogers Pass Lake are most readily reached from the north via the Rollins Pass Road and Rogers Pass. They can also be approached from the East Portal of the Moffat Tunnel. The season for this hike is from the middle of July through October. On the way to Rogers Pass on the Continental Divide, you are mostly above timberline and have great views, especially of the Winter Park Ski Area and of James Peak.

Getting There: From Berthoud Pass, drive north on U.S. 40 for 11.5 miles and turn right onto Rollins Pass Road, Number 149. Follow this excellent dirt road for 10.6 miles and park off-road at Riflesight Notch. En route to this point stay on the main road and keep straight at mile 3.7 and at mile 6.4. Regular cars can reach this point when the road is clear of snow from July through October.

The Hike: Begin south up a side road leading from Riflesight Notch. After 1.25 miles through the trees, you will pass tree line and the vistas really open up. Follow the main, old mining road generally south and then southeast and reach Rogers Pass at a sign 2.5 miles from the trailhead. James Peak is very impressive to the south-southeast, Heart Lake down to the north, and Rogers Pass Lake down to the east. Follow the road, which soon becomes a trail, down generally northeast for almost 1 mile to lovely Heart Lake. Angle over to the southeast 0.4 mile to smaller Rogers Pass Lake before ascending 750 feet back to Rogers Pass and your return to Riflesight Notch.

262

Hike Distance: 2.5 miles to Rogers Pass. 0.9 mile to Heart Lake, 0.4 mile to Rogers Pass Lake. Total 3.8 miles each way.

Hiking Time: Up to Rogers Pass in 70 minutes. Down to Heart Lake in 16 minutes. Over to Rogers Pass Lake in 8 minutes. Back in 70 minutes.

Starting Elevation: 11,160 feet

Highest Elevation: 11,870

Elevation Gain: 1,645 feet (includes 935 extra feet)

Trail: All the way

Relevant Maps: Trails Illustrated 103

Empire 7½ minute

East Portal 7½ minute

Gilpin County

Grand County Four

Arapaho National Forest

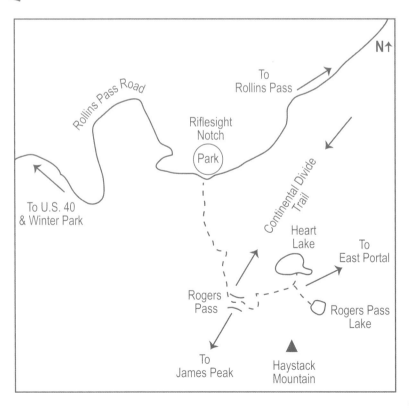

128 Cleveland Lake

Cleveland Lake lies above Holy Cross City, a ghost town that flourished between 1880 and 1884. Several cabins and many mining artifacts can be found in this town. Some old mines are evident along the road to the lake above Holy Cross City as well. From the upper parts of this hike there are excellent views of Mount of the Holy Cross to the north. The best time for this hike is from mid-July through late October.

Getting There: Drive on U.S. 24 either 9.7 miles north from Tennessee Pass or 12.7 miles south from I-70 at Exit 171 west of Vail. Turn west onto Homestake Road and set your odometer to zero. Continue on this good and wide road for 7.7 miles. Turn right at a signed fork onto Road 704. Keep right at another intersection at mile 9.9. The road gets a bit rougher; however, only adequate clearance and not four-wheel-drive is required. Keep right at the junction at mile 11 and descend slightly. At mile 11.8, the road turns to the left and ends 0.2 mile farther at a small waterfall of French Creek. Park here at the end of the road.

The Hike: Begin to the north-northeast on a narrow trail that ascends steeply to meet a rough four-wheel-drive road within 200 yards. Ascend to the left and follow this old mining road for 1.5 miles to a crossing of French Creek and a fork at a wooden sign. The right fork ascends to Fall Creek Pass; however, go left (southwest) into the trees. After another 0.25 mile pass a sign and wooden fencing along the left side of the road. In another 0.5 mile, the first mining artifacts can be seen on the right as the road bends sharply up and to the right. You are now in the area of Holy Cross City. Pass a road barrier and go right at a road intersection. (The left fork rises to Fancy Lake.) Within 100 yards, you reach another fork just before a second road barrier and several cabins. Ascend to the left (southwest) into the forest and follow this road past several old mines to eventually reach a ridge around timberline. The road then descends to the right another 0.3 mile to reach the outlet of Cleveland Lake. The Mount of the Holy Cross rises above to the north-northwest and Whitney Peak to the northeast. Enjoy this lovely setting before retracing your route back to the trailhead.

Hike Distance: 3.6 miles each way

Hiking Time: Up in 98 minutes. Down in 80 minutes.

Starting Elevation: 10,320 feet

Highest Elevation: 11,855 feet

Elevation Gain: 1,955 feet (includes 420 extra feet)

Trail: All the way

Relevant Maps: Trails Illustrated 126 or 149

Mount of the Holy Cross 7½ minute

Eagle County Number Four

White River National Forest

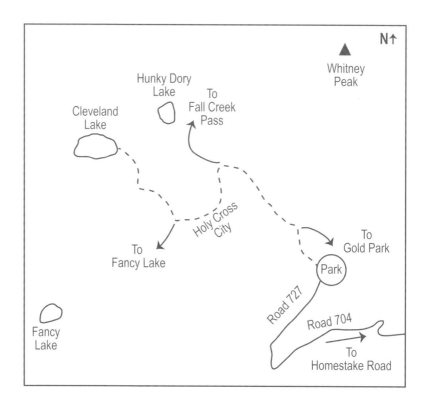

Bonus Hikes

The author just had to add more hikes (the man can't stop hiking!). These are not the hardest hikes in the book (hikes 1–128 are listed arbitrarily in order of increasing difficulty), but Dave wanted to add another hike in the Fort Collins area that he thought he had neglected. And he just couldn't pass up the chance to hike in Staunton State Park, which opened shortly before this book was ready for the printer.

129 Hewlett Gulch

The good trail up Hewlett Gulch follows Gordon Creek with many crossings (I counted 13) to a signed fork at the beginning of a loop. Named after an early settler, the gulch was later settled by the Spalding family, who built several cabins along the creek.

Getting There: From Fort Collins take U.S. 287 north 11 miles to CO 14. Turn left on CO 14 and travel 10.8 miles. Turn right on the bridge that crosses the Poudre River to the trailhead parking lot.

The Hike: Besides the many creek crossings as you meander up a pleasant valley, another reward is the view in all directions from the ridge top. Begin northwest and lose a little elevation, then ascend the gradual trail 2 miles to a signed fork. On your way, pass a stone cabin remnant. At the fork, rise to the left (northwest) and follow switchbacks up to the high point of a loop trail, which circles back to the signed fork. From this high point Livermore Mountain lies to the north, Greyrock Mountain is northeast, and North Bald Mountain is south-southwest in the distance. You may lengthen your trek by continuing the loop, but this description has you retracing your ascent route.

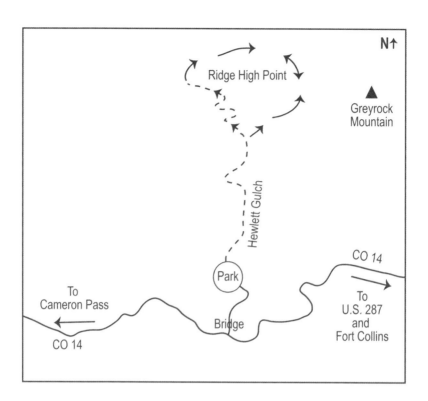

Hike Distance: 3 miles each way

Hiking Time: Up in 78 minutes. Down in 72 minutes.

Starting Elevation: 5,700 feet

Highest Elevation: 6,600 feet

Elevation Gain: 1,092 feet (includes 136 extra feet each way)

Trail: All the way

Relevant Maps: Trails Illustrated 101

    Poudre Park 7½ minute

    Larimer County Number Two

    Roosevelt National Forest

View from Staunton Rocks Overlook

Staunton State Park opened May 18, 2013. A gift of Frances H. Staunton, the park offers great rock formations, good trails, a picnic area, and lots of good scenery.

Getting There: From U.S. 285 between Conifer and Pine Junction, turn right (north) at Shaffers Crossing on Elk Creek Road and go 1.3 miles. Turn right into Staunton State Park, pay the entry fee, and park at the Ranch Hand group picnic area.

The Hike: Cross the road and begin east on the Staunton Ranch Trail. This trail curves slowly up to the Old Mill Trail after 1.8 miles. The cliffs and rocks are impressive. Ascend the Old Mill Trail on the right (north) for 0.9 mile to a trail junction at the wreckage of an old mill. Go left on the Border Line Trail for 1 mile to a signed fork and go left to the overlook. Enjoy the great vista before returning by your ascent route.

Hike Distance: 3.7 miles each way

Hiking Time: Up in 94 minutes. Down in 86 minutes.

Starting Elevation: 8,240feet

Highest Elevation: 9,4800 feet

Elevation Gain: 1,792 feet (includes 276 extra feet each way)

Trail: All the way

Relevant Maps: Staunton State Park (available at entrance)

Meridian Hill 7½ minute

Jefferson County Number Two

Pike National Forest

Views from the overlook: ESE to Long Scraggy Peak

S to Buffalo Mountain

SE to Little Scraggy Peak, Green Mountain, and Pikes Peak

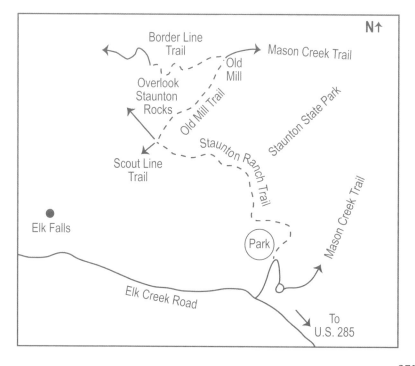

Hikes Listed by Nearest City

Idaho Springs

Jamestown

Jefferson

Keystone

LaPorte

Larkspur

Leadville

Littleton

Loveland

Lyons

Minturn

Monument

Morrison

Vail

Walden

Ward

Winter Park

Yampa

Index

Hikes described in this book are printed in **bold type**

About the Author

Dave Muller has been trekking in the Colorado high country for the past forty-four years. He has written six previous outdoor guides and for seventeen years wrote a weekly column in *The Denver Post*. A psychiatrist in private practice, Dave is from Washington, D.C., and after several years in Fort Worth, Texas, he rejoices that he moved his family to Colorado in 1969. Dave's wife, Jackie, is enjoying her new Steinway, which she received for *not* being mentioned in his last book.